McGraw-Hill's
CHINESE
ILLUSTRATED
DICTIONARY

New York Chicago San Francisco Lisbon London Madrid Mexico City
Milan New Delhi San Juan Seoul Singapore Sydney Toronto

1 2 3 4 5 6 7 8 9 10 11 12 13 14 15 16 17 18 19 20 21 CTP/CTP 0 9

ISBN 978-0-07-161590-7 (book and CD set)
MHID   0-07-161590-3 (book and CD set)

ISBN 978-0-07-161591-4 (book for set)
MHID   0-07-161591-1 (book for set)

Library of Congress Control Number: 2008935413

McGraw-Hill books are available at special quantity discounts to use as premiums and sales promotions or for use in corporate training programs. To contact a representative, please visit the Contact Us pages at www.mhprofessional.com.

MP3 Disk

The accompanying disk contains MP3 recordings of all terms presented in this dictionary. These files can be played on all MP3 players.
   For optimum use on the iPod:

1. Open iTunes on your computer.
2. Insert the disk into your computer and open via My Computer.
3. Drag the folder "Copy to iTunes Music Library" into Music in the iTunes menu. For older/slower computers, it is suggested that you first open this folder and drag the folders within to iTunes separately.
4. Sync your iPod with iTunes and eject the iPod.
5. Locate the recordings on your iPod by following this path:
   Main menu: **Menu**
   Music menu: **Artists**
   Artist menu: **Chinese Illustrated Dictionary**
6. If you experience difficulties, check the Read Me file on the disk.

Contents

How to Use This Book

It is suggested that you listen to the audio recordings when using this book. It will make your learning more efficient.

Category title shown in English

Unit title including English and simplified Chinese

Category title shown in simplified Chinese

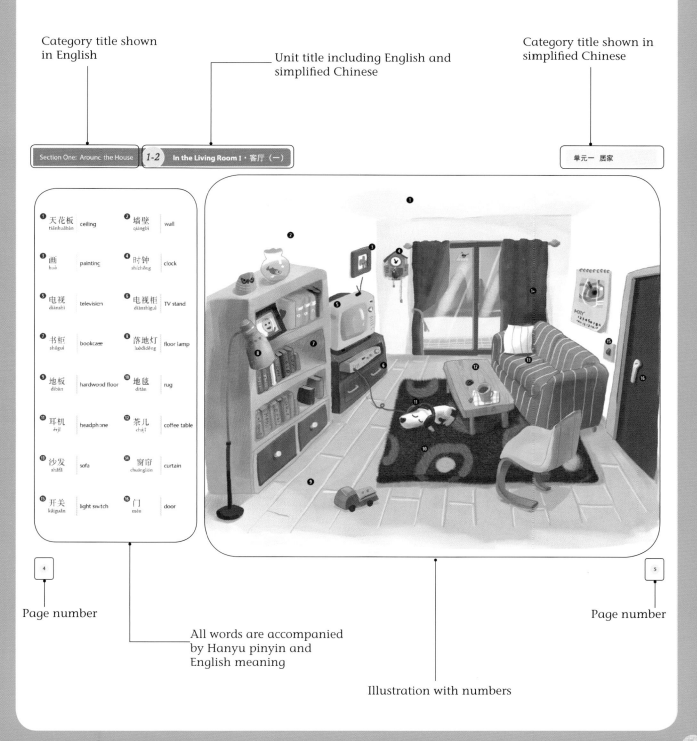

Section One: Around the House	**1-2**	**In the Living Room I · 客厅（一）**	单元一 居家

❶ 天花板 tiānhuābǎn ceiling
❷ 墙壁 qiángbì wall
❸ 画 huà painting
❹ 时钟 shízhōng clock
❺ 电视 diànshì television
❻ 电视柜 diànshìguì TV stand
❼ 书柜 shūguì bookcase
❽ 落地灯 luòdìdēng floor lamp
❾ 地板 dìbǎn hardwood floor
❿ 地毯 dìtǎn rug
⓫ 耳机 ěrjī headphone
⓬ 茶几 chájī coffee table
⓭ 沙发 shāfā sofa
⓮ 窗帘 chuānglián curtain
⓯ 开关 kāiguān light switch
⓰ 门 mén door

Page number

Page number

All words are accompanied by Hanyu pinyin and English meaning

Illustration with numbers

❶ 大楼 | building
dàlóu

❷ 铁窗 | iron window
tiěchuāng

❸ 游泳池 | swimming pool
yóuyǒngchí

❹ 大门 | main gate
dàmén

❺ 保安 | security guard
bǎo'ān

❻ 公寓 | apartment
gōngyù

❼ 阳台 | balcony
yángtái

❽ 顶楼 | top floor
dǐnglóu

⑨ 楼梯 lóutī | stair

⑩ 车库 chēkù | garage

⑪ 院子 yuànzi | yard

⑫ 信箱 xìnxiāng | mailbox

❶ 天花板
tiānhuābǎn | ceiling

❷ 墙壁
qiángbì | wall

❸ 画
huà | painting

❹ 时钟
shízhōng | clock

❺ 电视
diànshì | television

❻ 电视柜
diànshìguì | TV stand

❼ 书柜
shūguì | bookcase

❽ 落地灯
luòdìdēng | floor lamp

❾ 地板
dìbǎn | hardwood floor

❿ 地毯
dìtǎn | rug

⓫ 耳机
ěrjī | headphones

⓬ 茶几
chájī | coffee table

⓭ 沙发
shāfā | sofa

⓮ 窗帘
chuānglián | curtain

⓯ 开关
kāiguān | light switch

⓰ 门
mén | door

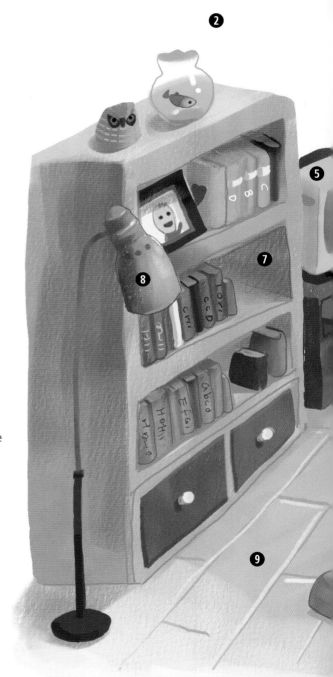

❶ 扶手椅 | armchair
fúshǒuyǐ

❷ 躺椅 | recliner
tǎngyǐ

❸ 摇椅 | rocking chair
yáoyǐ

❹ 小茶几 | end table
xiǎochájī

❺ 电话 | telephone
diànhuà

❻ 花瓶 | vase
huāpíng

❼ 垃圾桶 | trash can
lājītǒng

❽ 空调 | air conditioner
kōngtiáo

❾ 暖炉
nuǎnlú | space heater

❿ 电扇
diànshàn | fan

⓫ 音响
yīnxiǎng | stereo

⓬ DVD | DVD player

⓭ 遥控器
yáokòngqì | remote control

⓮ 吸尘器
xīchénqì | vacuum cleaner

⓯ 电话录音机
diànhuà lùyīnjī | answering machine

❶ 台式电脑 táishì diànnǎo	desktop computer	❷ 笔记本电脑 bǐjìběn diànnǎo	notebook computer	❸ CRT显示器 CRT-xiǎnshìqì	CRT monitor	❹ 液晶显示器 yèjīng xiǎnshìqì	LCD monitor
❺ 主板 zhǔbǎn	motherboard	❻ 中央处理器 zhōngyāng chǔlǐqì	CPU	❼ 内存 nèicún	RAM	❽ 硬盘 yìngpán	hard disk
❾ 网卡 wǎngkǎ	network adapter card	❿ 调制解调器 tiáozhì jiětiáoqì	modem	⓫ 鼠标 shǔbiāo	mouse	⓬ 鼠标垫 shǔbiāodiàn	mouse pad
⓭ 键盘 jiànpán	keyboard	⓮ 光驱 guāngqū	DVD-ROM drive	⓯ 光盘 guāngpán	DVD		

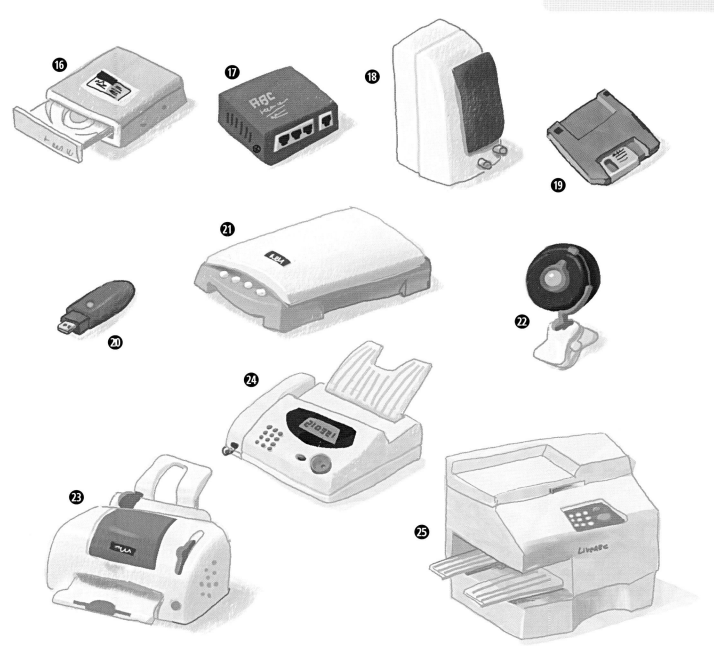

16 刻录机 kèlùjī | CD burner	**17** 集线器 jíxiànqì | hub	**18** 音箱 yīnxiāng | speaker	**19** 软盘 ruǎnpán | floppy disk
20 U盘 U-pán | flash drive	**21** 扫瞄仪 sǎomiáoyí | scanner	**22** 摄像头 shèxiàngtóu | webcam	**23** 打印机 dǎyìnjī | printer
24 传真机 chuánzhēnjī | fax machine	**25** 复印机 fùyìnjī | photocopier		

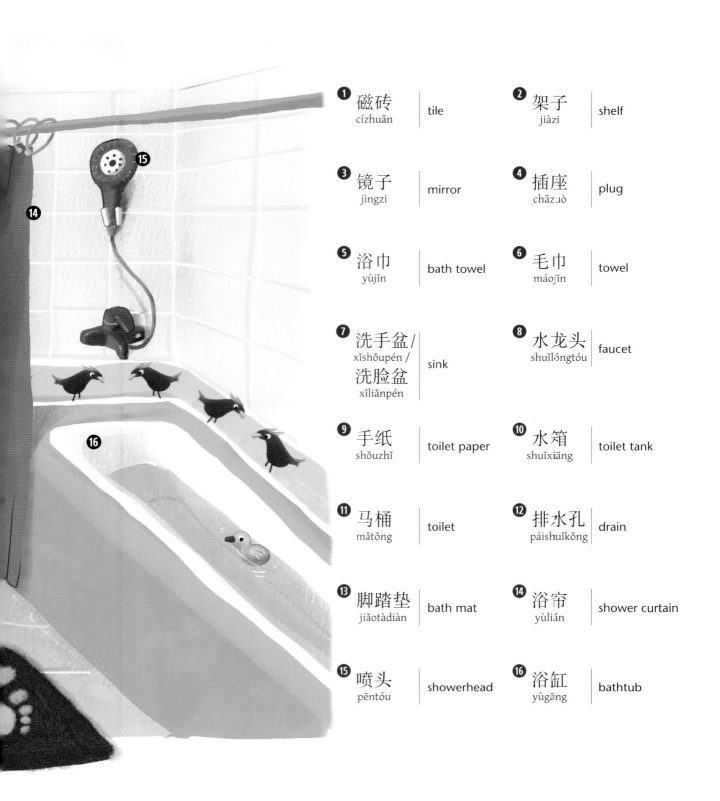

① 磁砖
cízhuān | tile

② 架子
jiàzi | shelf

③ 镜子
jìngzi | mirror

④ 插座
chāzuò | plug

⑤ 浴巾
yùjīn | bath towel

⑥ 毛巾
máojīn | towel

⑦ 洗手盆 /
xǐshǒupén /
洗脸盆
xǐliǎnpén | sink

⑧ 水龙头
shuǐlóngtóu | faucet

⑨ 手纸
shǒuzhǐ | toilet paper

⑩ 水箱
shuǐxiāng | toilet tank

⑪ 马桶
mǎtǒng | toilet

⑫ 排水孔
páishuǐkǒng | drain

⑬ 脚踏垫
jiǎotàdiàn | bath mat

⑭ 浴帘
yùlián | shower curtain

⑮ 喷头
pēntóu | showerhead

⑯ 浴缸
yùgāng | bathtub

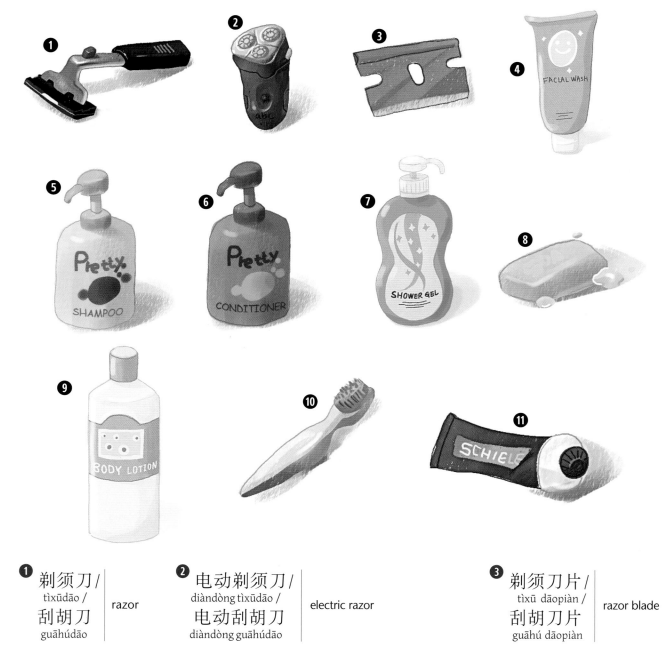

❶ 剃须刀 / tìxūdāo / 刮胡刀 guāhúdāo — razor

❷ 电动剃须刀 / diàndòng tìxūdāo / 电动刮胡刀 diàndòng guāhúdāo — electric razor

❸ 剃须刀片 / tìxū dāopiàn / 刮胡刀片 guāhú dāopiàn — razor blade

❹ 洗面奶 xǐmiànnǎi — facial wash

❺ 洗发水 / xǐfàshuǐ / 洗发液 xǐfàyè — shampoo

❻ 润发液 / rùnfàyè / 润发露 rùnfàlù — conditioner

❼ 沐浴液 mùyùyè — shower gel

❽ 香皂 xiāngzào — soap

❾ 润肤露 rùnfūlù — body lotion

❿ 牙刷 yáshuā — toothbrush

⓫ 牙膏 yágāo — toothpaste

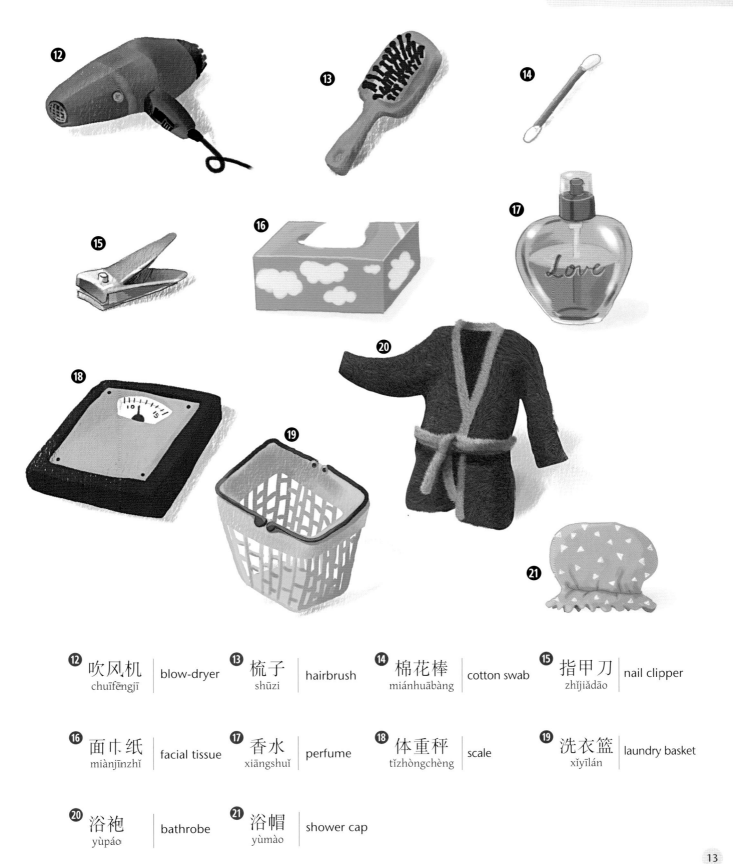

⑫ 吹风机 chuīfēngjī	blow-dryer	⑬ 梳子 shūzi	hairbrush

⑫ 吹风机 chuīfēngjī | blow-dryer　⑬ 梳子 shūzi | hairbrush　⑭ 棉花棒 miánhuābàng | cotton swab　⑮ 指甲刀 zhǐjiǎdāo | nail clipper

⑯ 面巾纸 miànjīnzhǐ | facial tissue　⑰ 香水 xiāngshuǐ | perfume　⑱ 体重秤 tǐzhòngchèng | scale　⑲ 洗衣篮 xǐyīlán | laundry basket

⑳ 浴袍 yùpáo | bathrobe　㉑ 浴帽 yùmào | shower cap

❶ 防晒油 | sunscreen
fángshàiyóu

❷ 隔离霜 | pre-makeup
gélíshuāng | cream

❸ 粉底液 | moisture
fěndǐyè | foundation

❹ 粉饼 | compact
fěnbǐng | foundation

❺ 眉笔 | eyebrow
méibǐ | pencil

❻ 眼影 | eye shadow
yǎnyǐng

❼ 眼线笔 | eye pencil
yǎnxiànbǐ

❽ 睫毛膏 | mascara
jiémáogāo

9 睫毛夹 | eyelash curler
jiémáojiá

10 腮红 | blush
sāihóng

11 刷子 | brush
shuāzi

12 口红 | lipstick
kǒuhóng

13 指甲油 | nail polish
zhǐjiǎyóu

14 卸妆油 | makeup remover
xièzhuāngyóu

15 面膜 | mask
miànmó

1 闹钟
nàozhōng | alarm clock

2 相框
xiàngkuàng | picture frame

3 台灯
táidēng | lamp

4 床头几
chuángtóujī | nightstand

5 床头柜
chuángtóuguì | headboard cabinet

6 枕头
zhěntou | pillow

7 双人床
shuāngrénchuáng | double bed

8 床垫
chuángdiàn | mattress

9 床单
chuángdān | sheet

10 被子
bèizi | comforter

11 拖鞋
tuōxié | slippers

12 汗衫
hànshān | undershirt

13 脚凳
jiǎodèng | footstool

14 五斗柜
wǔdǒuguì | chest of drawers

15 书档
shūdǎng | bookend

16 衣橱
yīchú | wardrobe

17 化妆品
huàzhuāngpǐn | cosmetics

18 梳妆台
shūzhuāngtái | vanity

Additional Information: Kinds of Beds

1. 单人床
dānrénchuáng | single bed

2. 沙发床
shāfāchuáng | sofa bed

1 洗衣液 | laundry detergent
xǐyīyè

2 柔顺剂 | fabric softener
róushùnjì

3 漂白粉 /
piǎobáifěn /
漂白液 | bleach
piǎobáiyè

4 衣架 | hanger
yījià

5 夹子 | clothes pin
jiázi

6 线 | thread
xiàn

7 烫衣板 | ironing board
tàngyībǎn

8 熨斗 | iron
yùndǒu

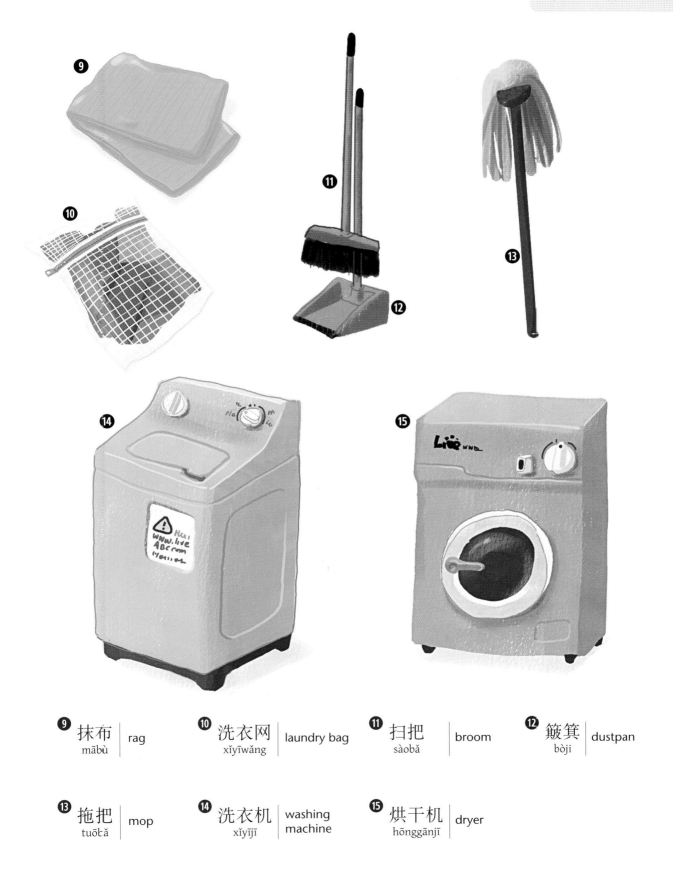

⑨ 抹布 mābù | rag

⑩ 洗衣网 xǐyīwǎng | laundry bag

⑪ 扫把 sàobǎ | broom

⑫ 簸箕 bòji | dustpan

⑬ 拖把 tuōbǎ | mop

⑭ 洗衣机 xǐyījī | washing machine

⑮ 烘干机 hōnggānjī | dryer

❶ 冰箱 | refrigerator
bīngxiāng

❷ 围裙 | apron
wéiqún

❸ 咖啡壶 | coffee maker
kāfēihú

❹ 抽油烟机 | range fan
chōuyóuyānjī

❺ 碗柜 | cupboard
wǎnguì

❻ 微波炉 | microwave oven
wēibōlú

❼ 碗架 | dish rack
wǎnjià

❽ 勺子 | ladle
sháozi

❾ 菜刀 | cleaver
càidāo

❿ 平底锅 | pan
píngdǐguō

⓫ 煤气炉 | gas stove
méiqìlú

⓬ 炒菜锅 | wok
chǎocàiguō

⓭ 水槽 | sink
shuǐcáo

⓮ 操作台 | counter
cāozuòtái

⓯ 菜板子 | cutting board
càibǎnzi

⓰ 烘碗机 | dish dryer
hōngwǎnjī

⓱ 烤箱 | oven
kǎoxiāng

⓲ 柜子 | cabinet
guìzi

⓳ 榨汁机 | blender
zhàzhījī

⓴ 电饭锅 | rice cooker
diànfànguō

㉑ 电热水壶 | electric water boiler
diànrèshuǐhú

㉒ 烤面包机 | toaster
kǎomiànbāojī

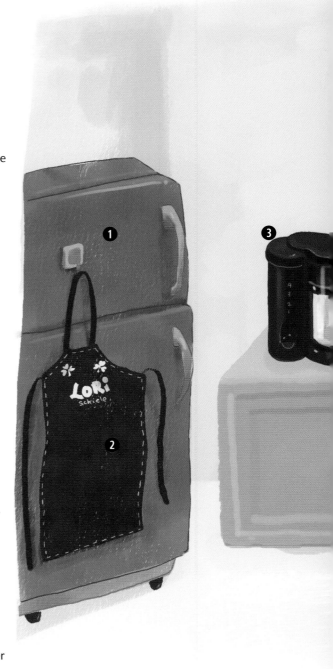

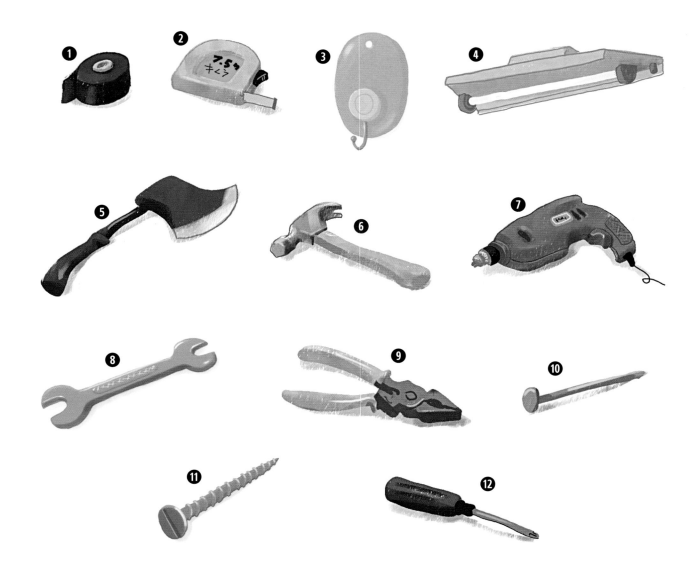

❶ 胶带 | tape
jiāodài

❷ 皮尺 | tape measure
píchǐ

❸ 挂钩 | hook
guàgōu

❹ 日光灯 | fluorescent light
rìguāngdēng

❺ 斧头 | ax
fǔtou

❻ 榔头 | hammer
lángtou

❼ 电钻 | electric drill
diànzuàn

❽ 扳手 | wrench
bānshou

❾ 钳子 | pliers
qiánzi

❿ 铁钉 | nail
tiědīng

⓫ 螺丝 | screw
luósī

⓬ 螺丝刀 | screwdriver
luósīdāo

⑬ 手电筒 shǒudiàntǒng	flashlight	⑭ 工具箱 gōngjùxiāng	toolbox	⑮ 油漆 yóuqī	paint	⑯ 油漆刷 yóuqīshuā	paintbrush
⑰ 油漆滚筒 yóuqī gǔntǒng	paint roller	⑱ 梯子 tīzi	ladder	⑲ 铲子 chǎnzi	shovel	⑳ 刷子 shuāzi	scrubbing brush
㉑ 水桶 shuǐtǒng	bucket	㉒ 海绵 hǎimián	sponge					

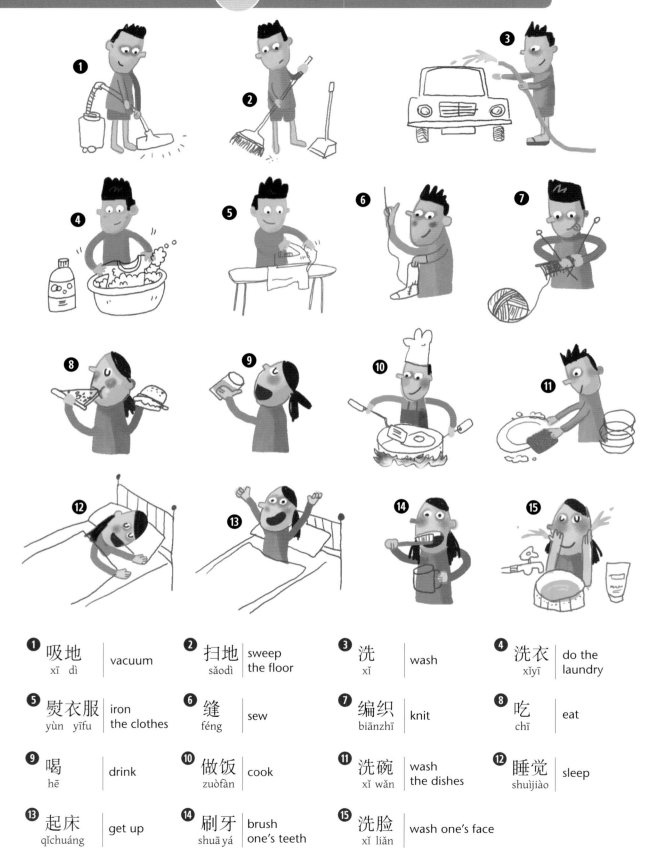

❶ 吸地 xī dì	vacuum	❷ 扫地 sǎodì	sweep the floor	❸ 洗 xǐ	wash	❹ 洗衣 xǐyī	do the laundry
❺ 熨衣服 yùn yīfu	iron the clothes	❻ 缝 féng	sew	❼ 编织 biānzhī	knit	❽ 吃 chī	eat
❾ 喝 hē	drink	❿ 做饭 zuòfàn	cook	⓫ 洗碗 xǐ wǎn	wash the dishes	⓬ 睡觉 shuìjiào	sleep
⓭ 起床 qǐchuáng	get up	⓮ 刷牙 shuā yá	brush one's teeth	⓯ 洗脸 xǐ liǎn	wash one's face		

⑯ 洗澡 xǐzǎo	take a shower	⑰ 穿 chuān	wear (clothing)	⑱ 戴 dài	wear (accessories)	⑲ 脱 tuō	take off
⑳ 打电话 dǎ diànhuà	make a phone call	㉑ 浇花 jiāo huā	water the plants	㉒ 倒垃圾 dào lājī	take out the garbage	㉓ 打开 dǎkāi	open / turn on
㉔ 关上 guānshàng	close / turn off						

❶ 男人 | man
nánrén

❷ 女人 | woman
nǚrén

❸ 老先生 | aged man
lǎoxiānsheng

❹ 老太太 | aged woman
lǎotàitai

❺ 中年人 | middle-ager
zhōngnián rén

6 男孩儿 boy
nánháir

7 女孩儿 | girl
nǚháir

8 青少年 | teenager
qīngshàonián

9 孕妇 | pregnant woman
yùnfù

10 幼儿 toddler
yòu'ér

11 小孩儿 | child
xiǎoháir

12 婴儿 | baby
yīng'ér

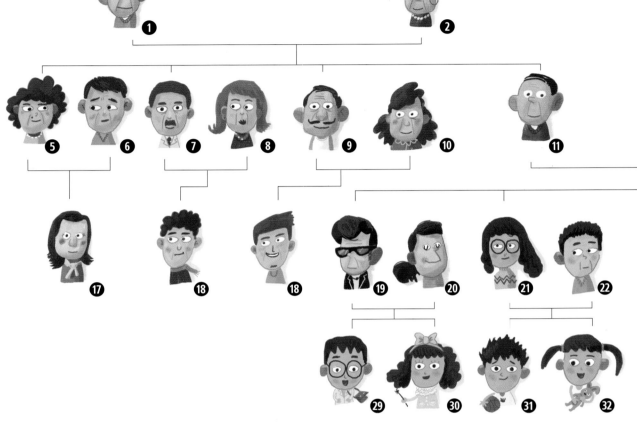

Father's side

❶ 祖父 / 爷爷
zǔfù / yéye | paternal grandfather

❷ 祖母 / 奶奶
zǔmǔ / nǎinai | paternal grandmother

❸ 外公
wàigōng | maternal grandfather

❹ 外婆
wàipó | maternal grandmother

❺ 姑姑
gūgu | aunt (father's sister)

❻ 姑父
gūfu | uncle (姑姑's husband)

❼ 叔叔
shūshu | uncle (father's younger brother)

❽ 婶婶
shěnshen | aunt (叔叔's wife)

❾ 伯父
bófù | uncle (father's elder brother)

❿ 伯母
bómǔ | aunt (伯父's wife)

⓫ 父亲 / 爸爸
fùqīn / bàba | father

⓬ 母亲 / 妈妈
mǔqīn / māma | mother

⓭ 舅舅
jiùjiu | uncle (mother's brother)

⓮ 舅妈
jiùmā | aunt (舅舅's wife)

⓯ 姨妈
yímā | aunt (mother's sister)

⓰ 姨丈
yízhàng | uncle (姨妈's husband)

⓱ 表哥 / 表姐 / 表弟 / 表妹
biǎogē / biǎojiě / biǎodì / biǎomèi | cousin (姑姑, 舅舅 and 姨妈's children)

⓲ 堂哥 / 堂姐 / 堂弟 / 堂妹
tánggē / tángjiě / tángdì / tángmèi | cousin (伯父 and 叔叔's children)

⓳ 哥哥
gēge | elder brother

⓴ 嫂子
sǎozi | sister-in-law (哥哥's wife)

28

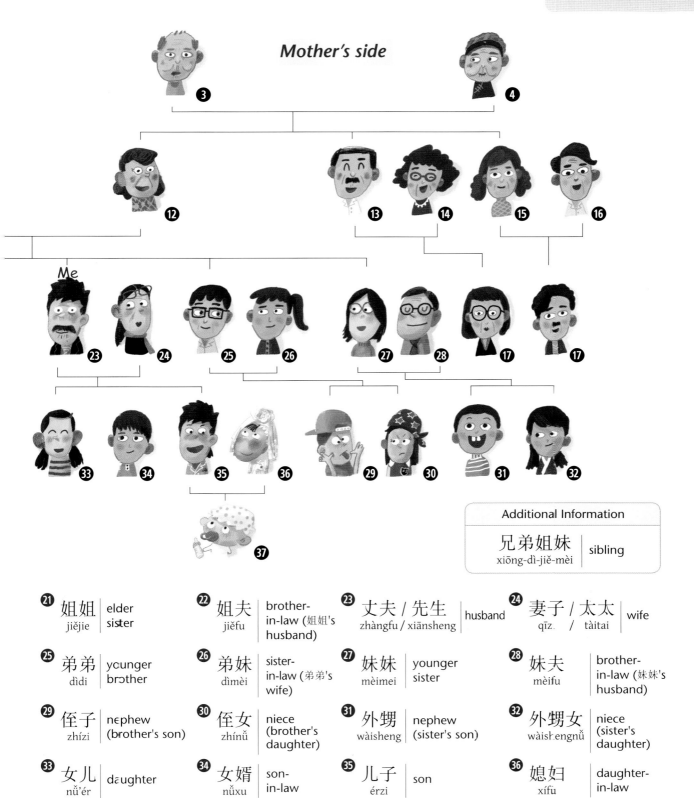

Mother's side

Me

Additional Information
兄弟姐妹 xiōng-dì-jiě-mèi │ sibling

㉑ 姐姐 jiějie │ elder sister

㉒ 姐夫 jiěfu │ brother-in-law (姐姐's husband)

㉓ 丈夫 / 先生 zhàngfu / xiānsheng │ husband

㉔ 妻子 / 太太 qīzi / tàitai │ wife

㉕ 弟弟 dìdi │ younger brother

㉖ 弟妹 dìmèi │ sister-in-law (弟弟's wife)

㉗ 妹妹 mèimei │ younger sister

㉘ 妹夫 mèifu │ brother-in-law (妹妹's husband)

㉙ 侄子 zhízi │ nephew (brother's son)

㉚ 侄女 zhínǚ │ niece (brother's daughter)

㉛ 外甥 wàisheng │ nephew (sister's son)

㉜ 外甥女 wàishengnǚ │ niece (sister's daughter)

㉝ 女儿 nǚ'ér │ daughter

㉞ 女婿 nǚxu │ son-in-law

㉟ 儿子 érzi │ son

㊱ 媳妇 xífu │ daughter-in-law

㊲ 孙子 sūnzi │ grandchild

❶ 业务员 yèwùyuán	salesman	❷ 助理 zhùlǐ	assistant	❸ 秘书 mìshū	secretary	❹ 经理 jīnglǐ	manager
❺ 记者 jìzhě	reporter	❻ 老师 lǎoshī	teacher	❼ 教授 jiàoshòu	professor	❽ 公务员 gōngwùyuán	public servant
❾ 警察 jǐngchá	policeman	❿ 消防员 xiāofángyuán	firefighter	⓫ 军人 jūnrén	soldier	⓬ 司机 sījī	driver

⑬ 飞行员 fēixíngyuán | pilot

⑭ 农民 nóngmín | farmer

⑮ 渔夫 yúfū | fisherman

⑯ 厨师 chúshī | chef

⑰ 建筑师 jiànzhùshī | architect

⑱ 技工 jìgōng | mechanic

⑲ 木匠 mùjiang | carpenter

⑳ 工人 gōngrén | laborer

㉑ 水电工 shuǐdiàngōng | plumber

❶ 医生
yīshēng | doctor

❷ 护士
hùshi | nurse

❸ 科学家
kēxuéjiā | scientist

❹ 工程师
gōngchéngshī | engineer

❺ 政治家
zhèngzhìjiā | politician

❻ 商人
shāngrén | businessman

❼ 企业家
qǐyèjiā | entrepreneur

❽ 律师
lùshī | lawyer

❾ 法官
fǎguān | judge

❿ 导游
dǎoyóu | tour guide

11 中介
zhōngjiè | broker / agent

12 男演员
nányǎnyuán | actor

13 女演员
nǚyǎnyuán | actress

14 歌手
gēshǒu | singer

15 发型设计师
fàxíng shèjìshī | hairstylist

16 艺术家
yìshùjiā | artist

17 音乐家
yīnyuèjiā | musician

18 舞蹈家
wǔdǎojiā | dancer

19 雕塑家
diāosùjiā | sculptor

20 运动员
yùndòngyuán | athlete

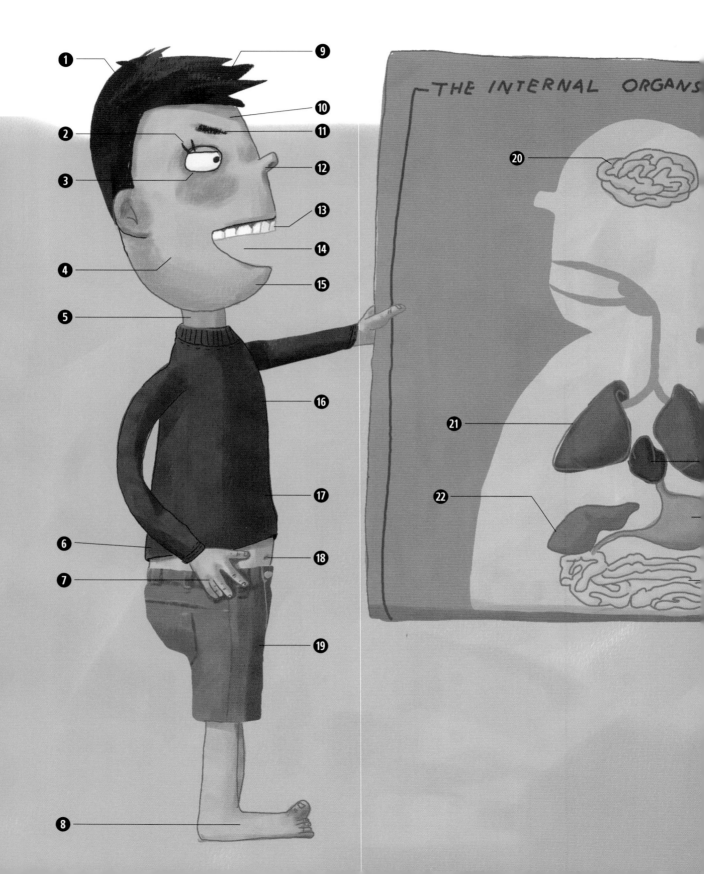

THE INTERNAL ORGANS

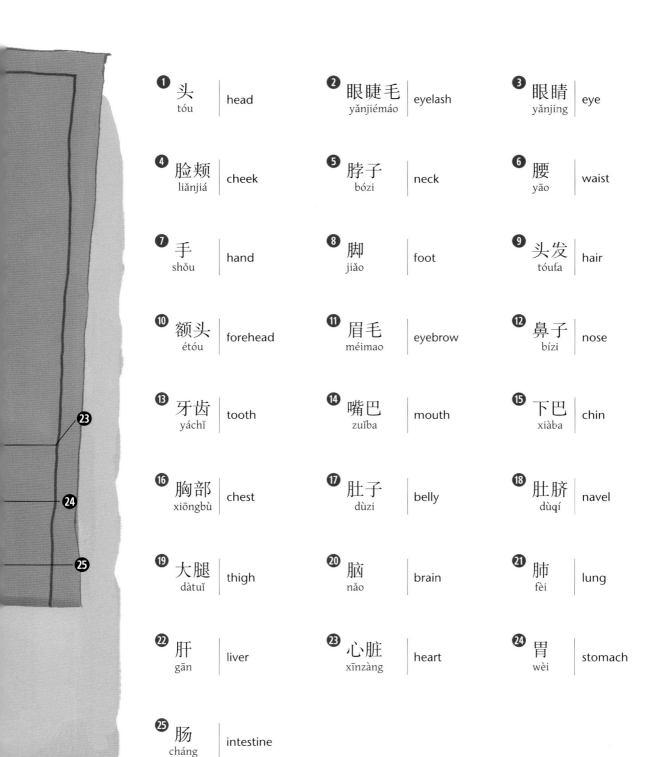

❶ 头 tóu | head

❷ 眼睫毛 yǎnjiémáo | eyelash

❸ 眼睛 yǎnjing | eye

❹ 脸颊 liǎnjiá | cheek

❺ 脖子 bózi | neck

❻ 腰 yāo | waist

❼ 手 shǒu | hand

❽ 脚 jiǎo | foot

❾ 头发 tóufa | hair

❿ 额头 étóu | forehead

⓫ 眉毛 méimao | eyebrow

⓬ 鼻子 bízi | nose

⓭ 牙齿 yáchǐ | tooth

⓮ 嘴巴 zuǐba | mouth

⓯ 下巴 xiàba | chin

⓰ 胸部 xiōngbù | chest

⓱ 肚子 dùzi | belly

⓲ 肚脐 dùqí | navel

⓳ 大腿 dàtuǐ | thigh

⓴ 脑 nǎo | brain

㉑ 肺 fèi | lung

㉒ 肝 gān | liver

㉓ 心脏 xīnzàng | heart

㉔ 胃 wèi | stomach

㉕ 肠 cháng | intestine

❶

❷

❸

❹

❺

❻

❶ 快乐 | happy
kuàilè

❷ 兴奋 | excited
xīngfèn

❸ 精力充沛 | energetic
jīnglì-chōngpèi

❹ 惊讶 | surprised
jīngyà

❺ 生气 | angry
shēngqì

❻ 尴尬 | embarrassed
gāngà

7

8

9

10

11

12

7 害羞 | shy
hàixiū

8 紧张 | nervous
jǐnzhāng

9 微笑 | smiling
wēixiào

10 笑 | laughing
xiao

11 哭 | crying
kū

12 疲倦 | tired
píjuàn

① 摔跤 | fall flat
shuāijiāo | on (one's) back

② 跌倒 | fall
diēdǎo

③ 站 | stand
zhàn

④ 跪 | kneel
guì

⑤ 蹲 | squat
dūn

⑥ 倒立 | do a
dàolì | handstand

⑦ 走 | walk
zǒu

⑧ 爬 | crawl
pá

❾ 跳 tiào	jump	❿ 踢 tī	kick	⓫ 坐 zuò	sit	⓬ 躺 tǎng	lie down

⓭ 趴 pā	lie face down	⓮ 背 bēi	carry (something) on (one's) back	⓯ 伸懒腰 shēnlǎnyāo	stretch

❶ 十字转门 shízì zhuànmén | turnstile

❷ 冷冻食品 lěngdòng shípǐn | frozen food

❸ 乳制品 rǔzhìpǐn | dairy products

❹ 饮料 yǐnliào | beverages

❺ 罐头(食品) guàntou(shípǐn) | canned food

❻ 包装食品 bāozhuāng shípǐn | packaged food

❼ 面包 miànbāo | bread

❽ 零食 língshí | snacks

❾ 购物袋儿 gòuwùdàir | shopping bag

❿ 试吃品 shìchīpǐn | free sample

⓫ 肉类 ròulèi | meat

⓬ 海鲜 hǎixiān | seafood

⓭ 篮子 lánzi | basket

⓮ 蔬菜 shūcài | vegetables

⓯ 水果 shuǐguǒ | fruit

⓰ 顾客 gùkè | customer

⓱ 手推车 shǒutuīchē | cart

⓲ 收款机 shōukuǎnjī | cash register

⓳ 条形码 tiáoxíngmǎ 扫描仪 sǎomiáoyí | scanner

⓴ 收银员 shōuyínyuán | cashier

㉑ 塑料袋儿 sùliàodàir | plastic bag

㉒ 现金 xiànjīn | cash

㉓ 收据 shōujù | receipt

㉔ 资源 zīyuán 回收桶 huíshōutǒng | recycling bin

㉕ 熟食 shúshí | deli food

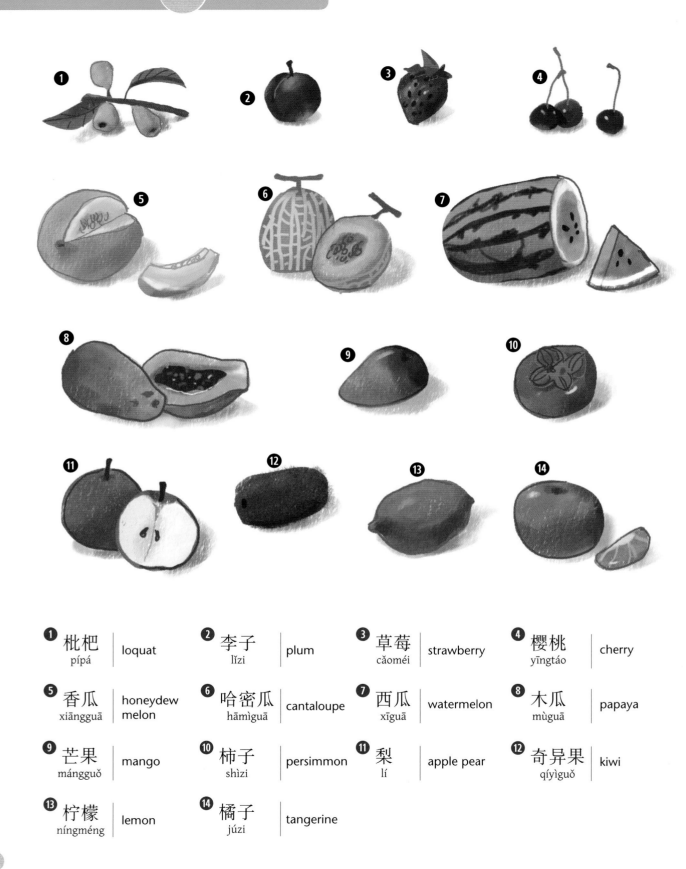

❶ 枇杷 pípá	loquat	❷ 李子 lǐzi	plum	❸ 草莓 cǎoméi	strawberry	❹ 樱桃 yīngtáo	cherry
❺ 香瓜 xiāngguā	honeydew melon	❻ 哈密瓜 hāmìguā	cantaloupe	❼ 西瓜 xīguā	watermelon	❽ 木瓜 mùguā	papaya
❾ 芒果 mángguǒ	mango	❿ 柿子 shìzi	persimmon	⓫ 梨 lí	apple pear	⓬ 奇异果 qíyìguǒ	kiwi
⓭ 柠檬 níngméng	lemon	⓮ 橘子 júzi	tangerine				

⑮ 橙子 chéngzi	orange	⑯ 葡萄柚 pútáoyòu	grapefruit	⑰ 葡萄 pútáo	grapes	⑱ 杨桃 yángtáo	starfruit
⑲ 苹果 píngguǒ	apple	⑳ 香蕉 xiāngjiāo	banana	㉑ 莲雾 liánwù	wax apple	㉒ 番石榴 fānshíliu	guava
㉓ 荔枝 lìzhī	lychee	㉔ 龙眼 lóngyǎn	longan	㉕ 榴莲 liúlián	durian	㉖ 菠萝 bōluó	pineapple

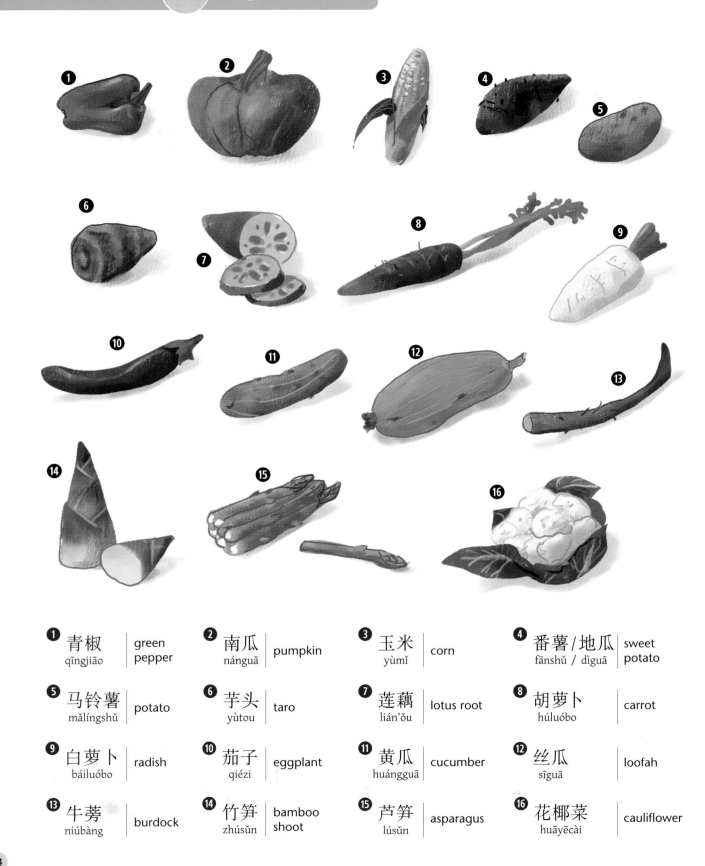

❶ 青椒 qīngjiāo | green pepper	**❷ 南瓜** nánguā | pumpkin	**❸ 玉米** yùmǐ | corn	**❹ 番薯 / 地瓜** fānshǔ / dìguā | sweet potato
❺ 马铃薯 mǎlíngshǔ | potato	**❻ 芋头** yùtou | taro	**❼ 莲藕** lián'ǒu | lotus root	**❽ 胡萝卜** húluóbo | carrot
❾ 白萝卜 báiluóbo | radish	**❿ 茄子** qiézi | eggplant	**⓫ 黄瓜** huángguā | cucumber	**⓬ 丝瓜** sīguā | loofah
⓭ 牛蒡 niúbàng | burdock	**⓮ 竹笋** zhúsǔn | bamboo shoot	**⓯ 芦笋** lúsǔn | asparagus	**⓰ 花椰菜** huāyēcài | cauliflower

⑰ 卷心菜 juǎnxīncài	cabbage	⑱ 生菜 shēngcài	lettuce	⑲ 大白菜 dàbáicài	Chinese cabbage	⑳ 豆芽菜 dòuyácài	bean sprouts
㉑ 芥兰 jièlán	Chinese kale	㉒ 空心菜 kōngxīncài	water spinach	㉓ 蘑菇 mógu	mushrooms	㉔ 蕃茄 fānqié	tomato
㉕ 芹菜 qíncài	celery	㉖ 洋葱 yángcōng	onion	㉗ 葱 cōng	green onions	㉘ 蒜 suàn	garlic
㉙ 姜 jiāng	ginger	㉚ 九层塔 jiǔcéngtǎ	basil					

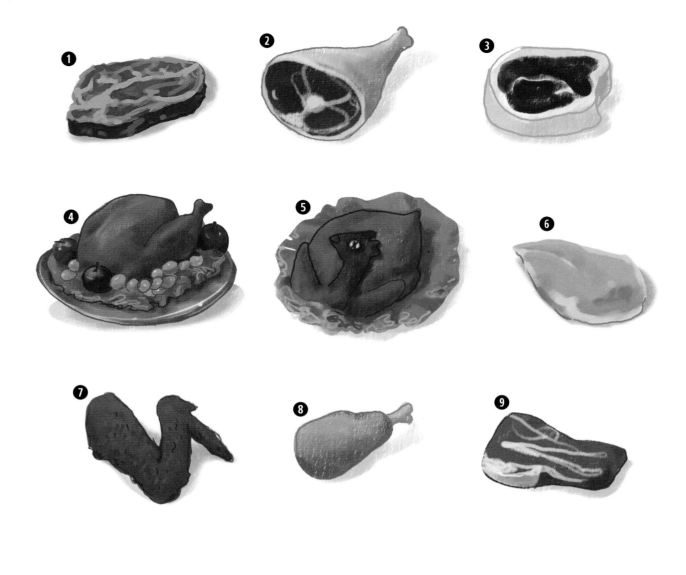

❶ 羊肉 | lamb
yángròu

❷ 小羊腿 | leg of lamb
xiǎoyángtuǐ

❸ 牛肉 | beef
niúròu

❹ 火鸡 | turkey
huǒjī

❺ 鸡肉 | chicken
jīròu

❻ 鸡胸肉 | chicken breast
jīxiōngròu

❼ 鸡翅 | chicken wing
jīchì

❽ 鸡腿 | chicken leg
jītuǐ

❾ 猪肉 | pork
zhūròu

❿ 肉馅
ròuxiàn | ground meat

⓫ 排骨
páigǔ | rib

⓬ 肉丸
ròuwán | meatball

⓭ 培根
péigēn | bacon

⓮ 火腿
huǒtuǐ | ham

⓯ 热狗
règǒu | hot dog

⓰ 香肠
xiāngcháng | sausage

⓱ 意大利腊肠
Yìdàlì làcháng | salami

⓲ 肉干儿
ròugānr | jerky

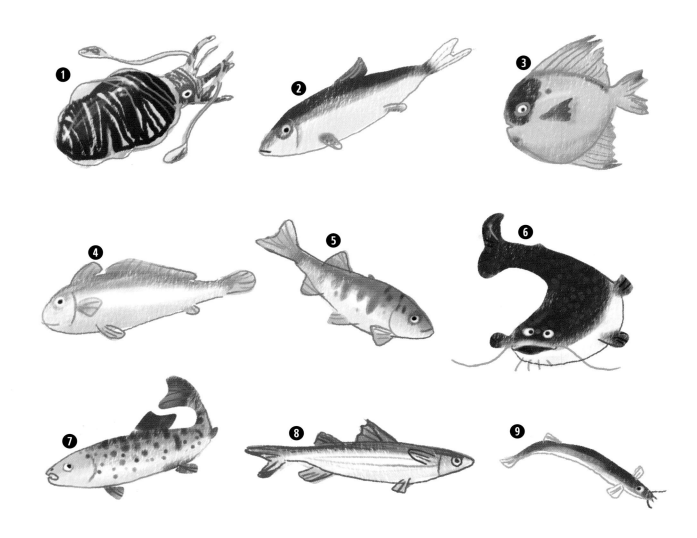

❶ 墨鱼 | cuttlefish
mòyú

❷ 遮目鱼 | milkfish
zhēmùyú

❸ 鲳鱼 | pomfret
chāngyú

❹ 黄鱼 | yellow croaker
huángyú

❺ 鳟鱼 | trout
zūnyú

❻ 鲶鱼 | catfish
niǎnyú

❼ 石斑鱼 | grouper
shíbānyú

❽ 乌鱼 | gray mullet
wūyú

❾ 泥鳅 | loach
níqiū

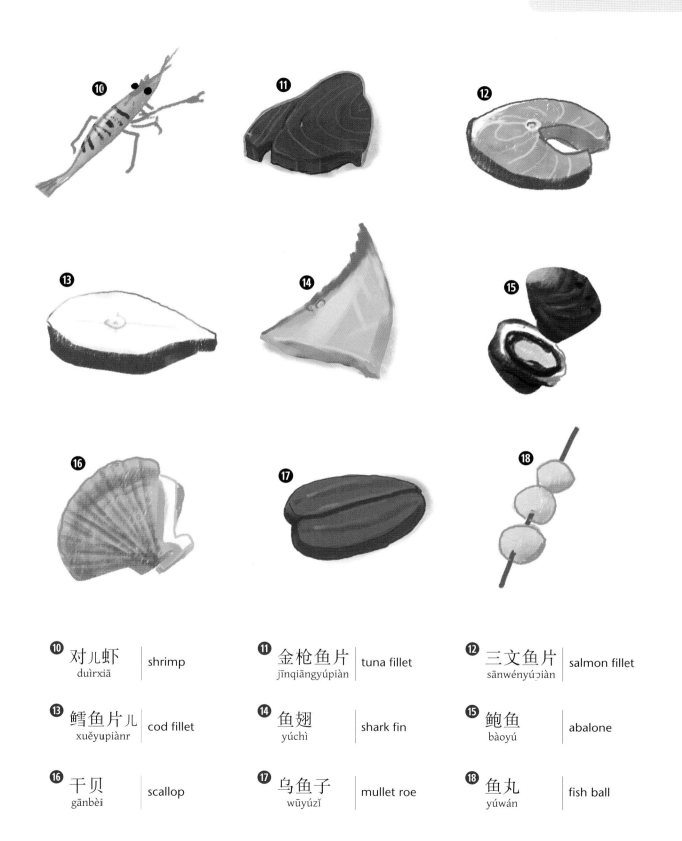

⑩ 对儿虾　| shrimp
duìrxiā

⑪ 金枪鱼片　| tuna fillet
jīnqiāngyúpiàn

⑫ 三文鱼片　| salmon fillet
sānwényúpiàn

⑬ 鳕鱼片儿　| cod fillet
xuěyupiànr

⑭ 鱼翅　| shark fin
yúchì

⑮ 鲍鱼　| abalone
bàoyú

⑯ 干贝　| scallop
gānbèi

⑰ 乌鱼子　| mullet roe
wūyúzǐ

⑱ 鱼丸　| fish ball
yúwán

❶ 可乐　| cola
kělè

❷ 沙士　| root beer
shāshì

❸ 汽水　| soda
qìshuǐ

❹ 冰沙　| smoothie
bīngshā

❺ 咖啡　| coffee
kāfēi

❻ 热巧克力　| hot chocolate
rèqiǎokèlì

❼ 乌龙茶　| oolong tea
wūlóngchá

❽ 绿茶　| green tea
lùchá

❾ 冰红茶　| iced tea
bīnghóngchá

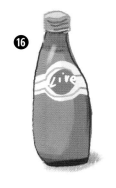

❿ 奶茶 nǎichá	milk tea

⓫ 珍珠奶茶 zhēnzhū nǎichá	bubble milk tea

⓬ 牛奶 niúnǎi	milk

⓭ 豆浆 dòujiāng	soybean milk

⓮ 米浆 mǐjiāng	brown rice milk

⓯ 有机饮料 yǒujī yǐnliào	organic drink

⓰ 矿泉水 kuàngquánshuǐ	mineral water

⓱ 柠檬水 níngméngshuǐ	lemonade

⓲ 果汁 guǒzhī	juice

❶ 黄油 huángyóu | butter

❷ 奶油 nǎiyóu | cream

❸ 冰淇淋 bīngqílín | ice cream

❹ 雪糕 xuěgāo | frozen treat

❺ 奶酪 nǎilào | cheese

❻ 酸奶 suānnǎi | yogurt / drinking yogurt / frozen yogurt

❼ 生奶油 shēngnǎiyóu | whipped cream

❽ 低脂牛奶 | low-fat milk
dīzhī niúnǎi

❾ 脱脂牛奶 | skim milk
tuōzhī niúnǎi

❿ 全脂牛奶 | whole milk
quánzhī niúnǎi

⓫ 奶粉 | powdered milk
nǎifěn

⓬ 炼乳 | condensed milk
liànrǔ

⓭ 奶昔 | milk shake
nǎixí

❶ 酸黄瓜 suānhuángguā	pickles	❷ 餐巾纸 / 纸巾 cānjīnzhǐ / zhǐjīn	paper napkins	❸ 吸管 xīguǎn	straw	❹ 打包袋 dǎbāodài	doggie bag
❺ 煎饼 jiānbǐng	pancakes	❻ 鸡块儿 jīkuàir	chicken nuggets	❼ 甜甜圈 tiántiánquān	doughnuts	❽ 洋葱圈 yángcōngquān	onion rings
❾ 牛角面包 niújiǎo miànbāo	croissant	❿ 带走 dàizǒu	to go	⓫ 凳子 dèngzi	stool	⓬ 汉堡 hànbǎo	hamburger

13 在这儿吃 | for here
zài zhèr chī

14 薯条 | french fries
shǔtiáo

15 餐盘 | serving tray
cānpán

16 百吉饼 | bagel
bǎijíbǐng

17 炸鸡 | fried
zhájī | chicken

18 松饼 | muffins
sōngbǐng

19 威化 | waffle
wēihuà

❶ 男服务生 | waiter
nánfúwùshēng

❷ 冰桶 | ice bucket
bīngtǒng

❸ 茶壶 | teapot
cháhú

❹ 咖啡壶 | coffeepot
kāfēihú

❺ 女服务生 | waitress
nǚfúwùshēng

❻ 桌布 | tablecloth
zhuōbù

❼ 菜单 | menu
càidān

❽ 盐瓶 | salt shaker
yánpíng

⑨ 账单 | bill
zhàngdān

⑩ 牙签 | toothpicks
yáqiān

⑪ 餐垫 | place mat
cāndiàn

⑫ 餐巾 | napkin
cānjīn

⑬ 领班 | hostess
lǐngbān

⑭ 柜台 | counter
guìtái

❶

❷

❸

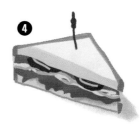
❹

❺

❻

❼

❽

❾

❿

❶ 开胃菜 | appetizer
　 kāiwèicài

❷ 沙拉 | salad
　 shālā

❸ 汤 | soup
　 tāng

❹ 三明治 | sandwich
　 sānmíngzhì

❺ 潜水艇三明治 | submarine sandwich
　 qiánshuǐtǐng sānmíngzhì

❻ 墨西哥饼 | taco
　 Mòxīgēbǐng

❼ 寿司 | sushi
　 shòusī

❽ 烤肉串 | shish kebab
　 kǎoròuchuàn

❾ 烤鸡 | roast chicken
　 kǎojī

❿ 牛排 | steak
　 niúpái

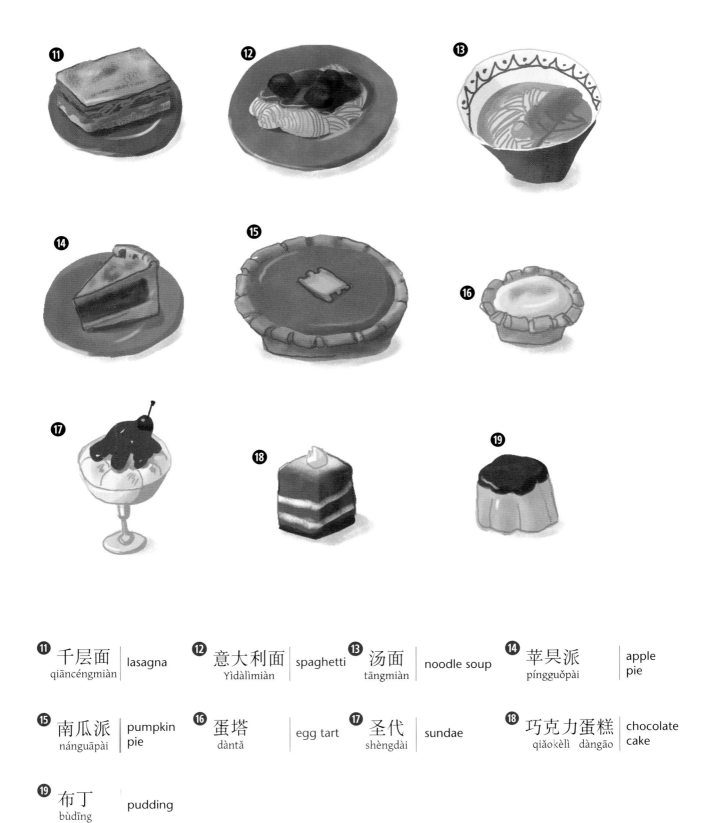

⓫ 千层面 qiāncéngmiàn | lasagna

⓬ 意大利面 Yìdàlìmiàn | spaghetti

⓭ 汤面 tāngmiàn | noodle soup

⓮ 苹果派 píngguǒpài | apple pie

⓯ 南瓜派 nánguāpài | pumpkin pie

⓰ 蛋塔 dàntǎ | egg tart

⓱ 圣代 shèngdài | sundae

⓲ 巧克力蛋糕 qiǎokèlì dàngāo | chocolate cake

⓳ 布丁 bùdīng | pudding

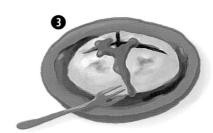

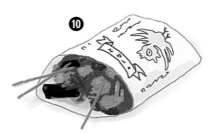

❶ 臭豆腐 chòudòufu	stinky tofu	❷ 炒米粉 chǎomǐfěn	fried rice noodles	❸ 肉圆 ròuyuán	fried steamed meat ball
❺ 鱼丸汤 yúwántāng	fish ball soup	❻ 蚵仔面线 kēzǎi miànxiàn	oyster noodles	❼ 肉羹面 ròugēngmiàn	pork with noodles in thick soup
❾ 卤味 lǔwèi	foods stewed with soy sauce	❿ 咸酥鸡 xiánsūjī	fried chicken with salt and pepper	⓫ 刨冰 bàobīng	ice shavings

10 Reasons to Go to Night Markets

You can't claim you've been to China until you've visited the night markets there. Night markets are like outdoor shopping malls chock full of local culture. Here are 10 reasons why you can't miss night markets in China:

1. Night markets are a food-lover's paradise. There is an endless supply of delicious edibles everywhere you turn. Some night markets are even famous for a particular dish. Since the portions are small, you can snack on as many different kinds of foods as you like before filling up.

2. If you're a cheapskate, night markets offer bargains galore. After all, who doesn't want to save a buck or two? The rows of colorful stands sell everything from watches to stereos to warm woolen mittens — and you just can't beat the price.

3. Goods at night markets are not only cheaper but also negotiable. Never stop at the price on the tag. Vendors always hike up their prices and they expect to be talked down. It can be a lot of fun to haggle, and it's satisfying too.

4. Slaves to fashion, look no further. Night markets stock the most current fashion trends at the best prices. It's a great place to breath new life into your wardrobe.

5. Where else but at a night market can you sample a plate of exotic seahorses and silkworm larvae? Enough said!

6. When you need a break from shopping and eating, stop off at one of the many game stands. All the classics are offered: pinball, balloon darts, and ring-toss. Sometimes you can win a goldfish.

7. Since you have to walk from stand to stand, you can burn up the calories from all the food you ate — and then eat more!

8. Night markets are good for those of us who like to stay up late and prefer the hustle-bustle of a noisy crowd to staying home. The lively atmosphere will stamp out feelings of boredom or loneliness.

9. Night market food is twenty times better than frozen microwave food from the convenience store, and the stands are open all night.

10. Last but not least, you can practice your Mandarin with vendors at the night markets. Don't forget to use the words you have learned from this book!

④ 卤肉饭 lǔròufàn	stewed minced pork served over rice
⑧ 牛肉面 niúròumiàn	beef noodles
⑫ 糖葫芦 tánghúlu	sugarcoated tomatoes on a stick

❶ 北京烤鸭 | Beijing
Běijīng kǎoyā | roast duck

❷ 宫保鸡丁 | Kung Pao
gōngbǎo jīdīng | chicken

❸ 红烧狮子头 | stewed
hóngshāo shīzitóu | pork balls

❺ 鱼香肉丝 | shredded pork
yúxiāng ròusī | with garlic sauce

❻ 麻婆豆腐 | Mapo tofu
mápó dòufu |

❼ 干扁四季豆 | fried beans,
gānbiǎn sìjìdòu | Sichuan style

❾ 火锅 | hot pot
huǒguō |

❿ 点心 | Dim Sum
diǎnxīn |

⓫ 饺子 | dumplings
jiǎozi |

⓭ 小笼包 | steamed
xiǎolóngbāo | pork dumplings

⓮ 酸辣汤 | hot and
suānlàtāng | sour soup

❹

❽

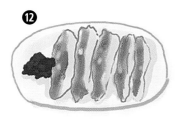

❶❷

❹ **糖醋排骨**
tángcù páigǔ | sweet and sour spare ribs

❽ **佛跳墙**
fótiàoqiáng | Buddha jumps over the wall

❶❷ **锅贴**
guōtiē | fried dumplings / pot stickers

Cultural Window

Chinese Meal Etiquette

Chinese people place great value on what they eat. They do not only put emphasis on the choice of ingredients but also on table manners. Table manners are a vital component and cannot be neglected if you want to understand Chinese culture. Let's have a look at what you need to know while dining and the arrangement of seats.

Seating Manners

The seating arrangement is a very important part of dining etiquette in China. One important concept is showing respect for elders and guests of honor. Normally, the rule is as follows: the left or eastern seat is reserved for the most respected person. This person also "faces the main entrance." After all of the guests have arrived and are ready to sit down and eat, we should remember that the oldest person is usually "the most respected person." Guests wait for this person to be seated first.

Female guest of honor   Male guest of honor
❶   ❶
Male guest ❷   ❸ Female guest
Female guest ❷   ❸ Male guest
❹   ❹
Hostess   Host

Things you need to know while dining

If you have a chance to eat with Chinese people, don't forget the following rules:

1. Don't eat until the elders or guests start.

2. Don't drink the soup from noodle soup directly from the bowl, and don't make noise while you are having soup.

3. Don't reach across the table to get food. You can use the rotatable board or ask the people who are close to the dish for help.

4. The bowl should be held and carried upright while eating. Do not put the bowl on the table or move your head toward it to eat.

5. Chinese people use chopsticks while eating. There are lots of rules you should know: First, don't use your chopsticks to gesture. Second, don't touch food with your chopsticks that you are not going to eat. Third, don't stick your chopsticks into the rice. Chinese people only do that to serve rice to spirits of people who have passed away. Fourth, don't tap your bowl with chopsticks. In old times, only the beggars on the street did that to gain attention in hopes someone would fill the empty bowl.

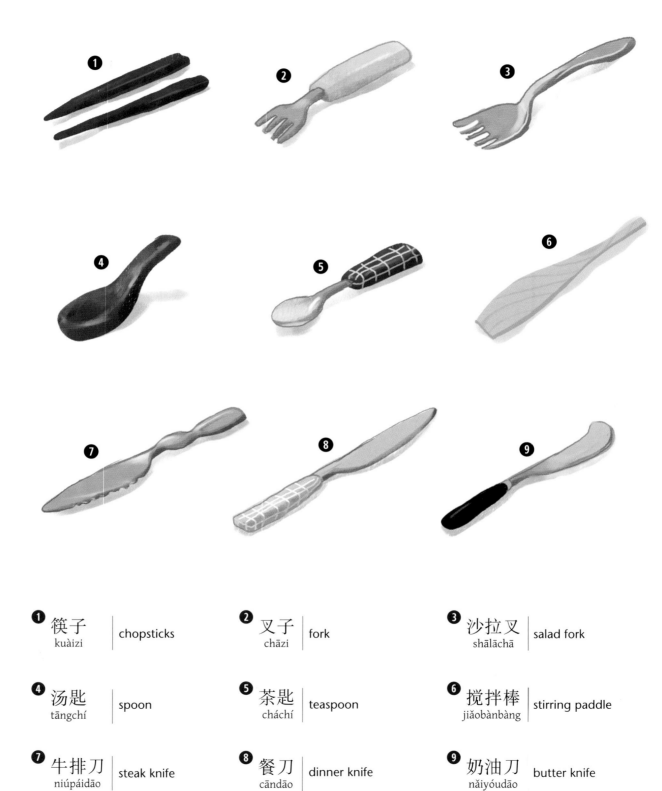

❶ 筷子 | chopsticks
kuàizi

❷ 叉子 | fork
chāzi

❸ 沙拉叉 | salad fork
shālāchā

❹ 汤匙 | spoon
tāngchí

❺ 茶匙 | teaspoon
cháchí

❻ 搅拌棒 | stirring paddle
jiǎobànbàng

❼ 牛排刀 | steak knife
niúpáidāo

❽ 餐刀 | dinner knife
cāndāo

❾ 奶油刀 | butter knife
nǎiyóudāo

 ❿

 ⓫

 ⓬

 ⓭

 ⓮

 ⓯

 ⓰

❿ 碗 | bowl
wǎn

⓫ 大浅盘 | platter
dàqiǎnpán

⓬ 盘子 | plate
pánzi

⓭ 碟子 | saucer
diézi

⓮ 水杯 | water glass
shuǐbēi

⓯ 烛台 | candlestick
zhútái

⓰ 蜡烛 | candle
làzhú

❶ 烤 kǎo	bake	❷ 火烤 huǒkǎo	grill	❸ 烧烤 shāokǎo	barbecue	❹ 炸 zhá	deep-fry
❺ 炒 chǎo	stir-fry	❻ 煎 jiān	fry	❼ 熬 áo	simmer	❽ 煮 zhǔ	boil
❾ 烫 tàng	blanch	❿ 炖 dùn	stew	⓫ 蒸 zhēng	steam		

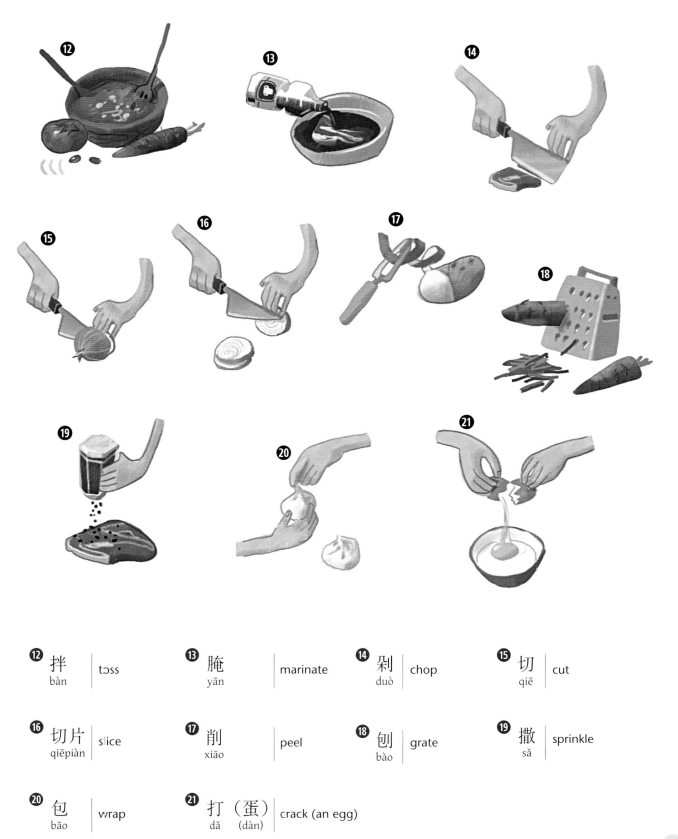

⓬ 拌 bàn — toss	**⓭ 腌** yān — marinate	**⓮ 剁** duò — chop	**⓯ 切** qiē — cut
⓰ 切片 qiēpiàn — slice	**⓱ 削** xiāo — peel	**⓲ 刨** bào — grate	**⓳ 撒** sǎ — sprinkle
⓴ 包 bāo — wrap	**㉑ 打（蛋）** dǎ (dàn) — crack (an egg)		

❶ 冰糖 | rock candy
bīngtáng

❷ 砂糖 | brown sugar
shātáng

❸ 盐 | salt
yán

❹ 胡椒 | pepper
hújiāo

❺ 味精 | MSG (monosodium glutamate)
wèijīng

❻ 柴鱼片 | dry bonito shavings
cháiyúpiàn

❼ 醋 | vinegar
cù

❽ 米酒 | rice wine
mǐjiǔ

❾ 色拉油 | cooking oil
sèlāyóu

❿ 橄榄油 | olive oil
gǎnlǎnyóu

⑪ 酱油 jiàngyóu	soy sauce	⑫ 香油 xiāngyóu	sesame oil	⑬ 玉米淀粉 yùmǐ diànfěn	corn starch	⑭ 太白粉 tàibáifěn	potato starch

⑪ 酱油 jiàngyóu | soy sauce

⑫ 香油 xiāngyóu | sesame oil

⑬ 玉米淀粉 yùmǐ diànfěn | corn starch

⑭ 太白粉 tàibáifěn | potato starch

⑮ 咖哩 gālí | curry

⑯ 味噌 wèizēng / wèicēng | miso

⑰ 芥末 jièmo | mustard

⑱ 蕃茄酱 fānqiéjiàng | ketchup

⑲ 辣椒酱 làjiāojiàng | chili sauce

⑳ 沙茶酱 shāchájiàng | shacha sauce

Additional Information

| 味噌 wèizēng / wèicēng | "味噌" is a loan word. It's pronounced as "wèizēng" in oral speaking. However, the pronunciation "zēng" does not appear in dictionaries, and some dictionaries indicate that the words "味噌" should be pronounced "wèicēng." |

❶ 连衣裙 liányīqún | dress	**❷ 礼服** lǐfú | gown	**❸ 套装** tàozhuāng | suit	**❹ 衬衫** chènshān | shirt
❺ 背心 bèixīn | vest	**❻ T恤** T-xù | T-shirt	**❼ 裙子** qúnzi | skirt	**❽ 裤子** kùzi | pants
❾ 牛仔裤 niúzǎikù | jeans	**❿ 短裤** duǎnkù | shorts		

⑪ 四角裤 | boxers
sìjiǎokù

⑫ 毛衣 | sweater
máoyī

⑬ 外套 | jacket
wàitào

⑭ 羽绒外套 | down coat
yǔróng wàitào

⑮ 运动服 | sportswear
yùndòngfú

⑯ 制服 | uniform
zhìfú

⑰ 雨衣 | raincoat
yǔyī

⑱ 睡衣 | pajamas
shuìyī

⑲ 胸罩 | bra
xiōngzhào

⑳ 内裤 | underwear
nèikù

❶ 帽子 | hat
màozi

❷ 头巾 | bandana
tóujīn

❸ 发带 | hair band
fàdài

❹ 发夹 | hair clip
fàjiá

❺ 耳环 | earrings
ěrhuán

❻ 面纱 | veil
miànshā

❼ 眼镜 | eyeglasses
yǎnjìng

❽ 墨镜 | sunglasses
mòjìng

❾ 皮包 | purse
píbāo

❿ 钱包 | wallet
qiánbāo

⓫ 背包 | backpack
bēibāo

⓬ 围巾 | scarf
wéijīn

⓭ 丝巾 | silk scarf
sījīn

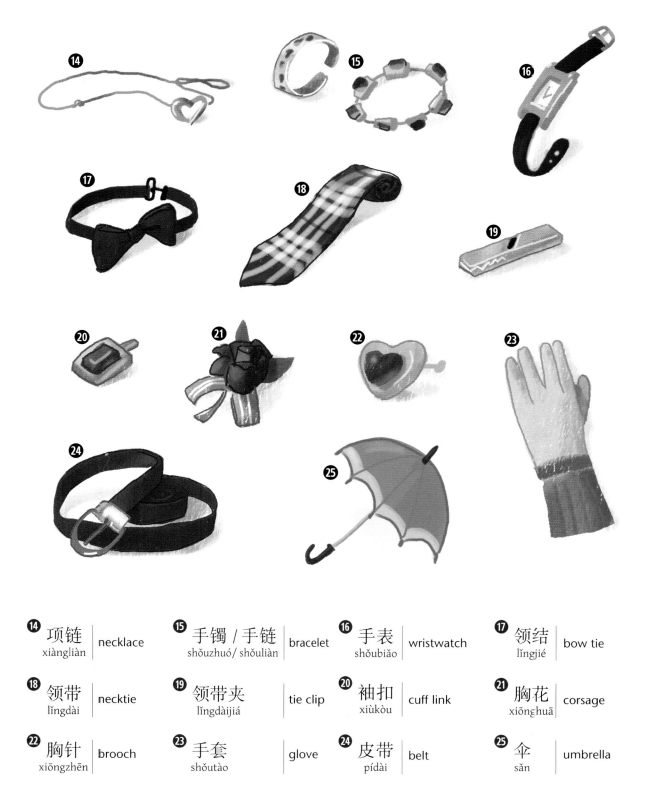

14 项链 xiàngliàn	necklace	**15** 手镯 / 手链 shǒuzhuó/ shǒuliàn	bracelet	**16** 手表 shǒubiǎo	wristwatch	**17** 领结 lǐngjié	bow tie
18 领带 lǐngdài	necktie	**19** 领带夹 lǐngdàijiá	tie clip	**20** 袖扣 xiùkòu	cuff link	**21** 胸花 xiōnghuā	corsage
22 胸针 xiōngzhēn	brooch	**23** 手套 shǒutào	glove	**24** 皮带 pídài	belt	**25** 伞 sǎn	umbrella

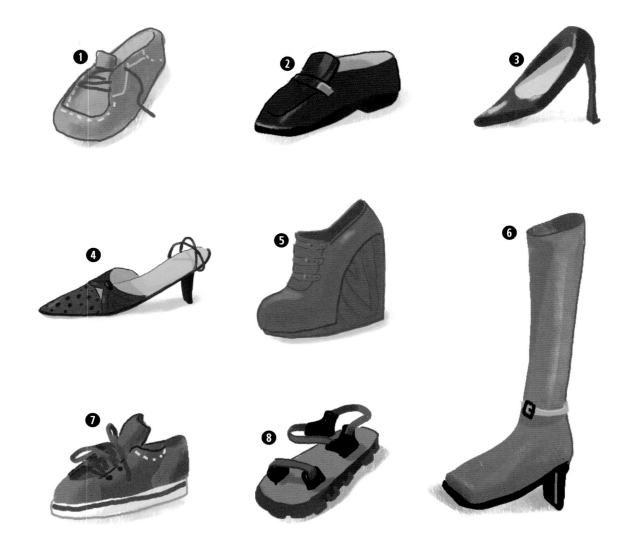

❶ 鞋子 | shoes
xiézi

❷ 皮鞋 | leather shoes
píxié

❸ 高跟鞋 | high-heeled shoes
gāogēnxié

❹ 尖头鞋 | pointed shoes
jiāntóuxié

❺ 厚底鞋 | platform shoes
hòudǐxié

❻ 靴子 | boots
xuēzi

❼ 运动鞋 | sneakers
yùndòngxié

❽ 凉鞋 | sandals
liángxié

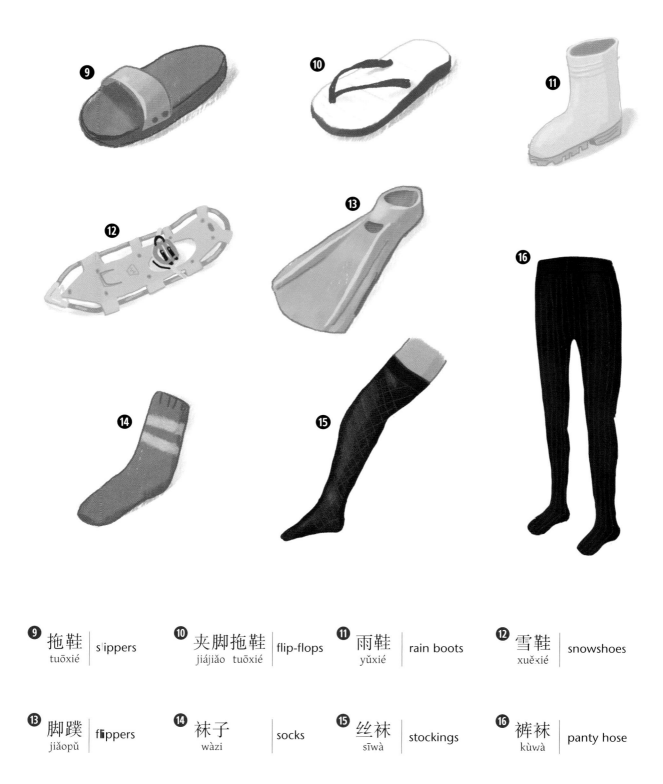

⑨ 拖鞋
tuōxié | slippers

⑩ 夹脚拖鞋
jiájiǎo　tuōxié | flip-flops

⑪ 雨鞋
yǔxié | rain boots

⑫ 雪鞋
xuěxié | snowshoes

⑬ 脚蹼
jiǎopǔ | flippers

⑭ 袜子
wàzi | socks

⑮ 丝袜
sīwà | stockings

⑯ 裤袜
kùwà | panty hose

❶ 旗袍 | cheongsam
qípáo

❷ 肚兜 | Chinese halter top
dùdōu

❸ 绣花鞋 | embroidered shoes
xiùhuāxié

❹ 棉袄 | cotton-padded jacket
mián'ǎo

❺ 长袍 | robe
chángpáo

❻ 唐装 | Tang suit
tángzhuāng

❼ 中山装
zhōngshānzhuāng | Chinese tunic suit

Cultural Window

The Image of Chinese Women – Cheongsam

Cheongsam is the first thing that would come to mind when it comes to Chinese costumes, regardless of whether you are Chinese or not. The cheongsam has become a symbol of traditional Chinese women. Nowadays, it integrates Chinese culture with influences from the West.

History of the Cheongsam

The cheongsam emerged after the Manchu invaded China in the 17th century. At this time, in order for the Manchu government to rule the Han people, many laws were created; one was that all women were required to wear a cheongsam. In the beginning, cheongsam were very simple, loose, and much different than they are today. Near the end of the Qing Dynasty (1644 – 1911), the sleeves and waist of the cheongsam were narrowed. The biggest change to the cheongsam occurred in the 1940s and is attributed to the impact of western culture, when the dresses became even slimmer to emphasize women's figures even more. Today, the cheongsam is worn by women all over the world on more formal occasions and often serve as evening gowns or even wedding gowns.

Fashion Inspiration

Though many people still love the traditional costumes of the past, they are not always suitable for a modern lifestyle. With the cheongsam, for example, the biggest disadvantage is that it can be somewhat physically limiting and cause certain actions to be difficult to perform. Therefore, many changes have been made to make it more comfortable and convenient to wear. Some of these changes have also been made for aesthetic reasons and often reflect a merging of eastern and western fashion design. These new creations can be very popular with young people and considered trendy all over the world.

With the influence of western culture, many western grand designers like to introduce the style of cheongsam into their designs. For example:

- an overlapped collar design with the left piece on top of the right piece;
- a split on the side from thigh to leg.

An introduction of these features into western design has introduced a new fashion trend to the market. Although the cheongsam has become less and less common in eastern culture, the cheongsam design is still a valuable piece of inspiration to designers everywhere, resulting in more fashionable products that combine western and eastern culture.

❶ 百货公司
bǎihuò gōngsī | department store

❷ KTV | karaoke bar

❸ 电器城
diànqìchéng | appliance store

❹ 便利商店
biànlì shāngdiàn | convenience store

❺ 饭馆
fànguǎn | restaurant

❻ 银行
yínháng | bank

❼ 医院
yīyuàn | hospital

❽ 邮局
yóujú | post office

❾ 自动售货机
zìdòng shòuhuòjī | vending machine

❿ 饭店
fàndiàn | hotel

⓫ 健身房
jiànshēnfáng | gym

⓬ 书店
shūdiàn | bookstore

⓭ 家具城
jiājùchéng | furniture store

⓮ 摊子
tānzi | street vendor's stall

⑮ 酒吧 jiǔbā	nightclub	⑯ 茶馆 cháguǎn	tea house	⑰ 咖啡店 kāfēidiàn	coffee shop	⑱ 药店 yàodiàn	pharmacy
⑲ 电影院 diànyǐngyuàn	movie theater	⑳ 警察局 jǐngchájú	police station	㉑ 玩具店 wánjùdiàn	toy store	㉒ 面包店 miànbāodiàn	bakery
㉓ 美容院 měiróngyuàn	beauty salon	㉔ 熟食店 shúshídiàn	delicatessen	㉕ 消防栓 xiāofángshuān	fire hydrant		

❶ 邮差 yóuchāi	mailman	❷ 邮筒 yóutǒng	mail drop	❸ 包裹 bāoguǒ	package	❹ 快递 kuàidì	express mail
❺ 信件 xìnjiàn	letter	❻ 寄信人地址 jìxìnrén dìzhǐ	return address	❼ 邮戳 yóuchuō	postmark	❽ 信封 xìnfēng	envelope
❾ 邮票 yóupiào	stamp	❿ 挂号信 guàhàoxìn	registered mail	⓫ 收信人地址 shōuxìnrén dìzhǐ	recipient's address	⓬ 邮政编码 yóuzhèng biānmǎ	zip code

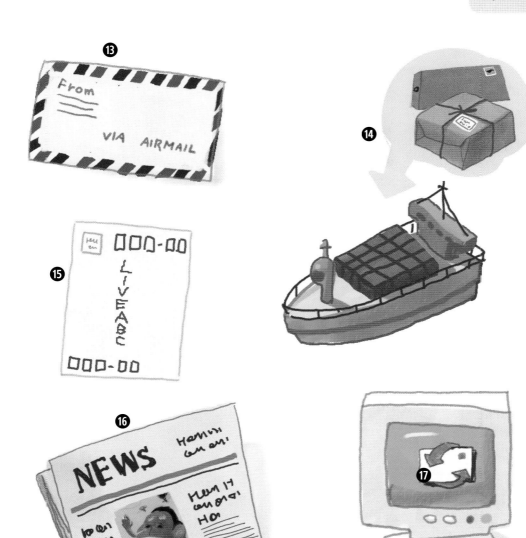

⑬ 航空信
hángkōngxìn | airmail

⑭ 海运
hǎiyùn | sea mail

⑮ 明信片
míngxìnpiàn | postcard

⑯ 报纸
bàozhǐ | newspaper

⑰ 电子邮件
diànzǐ yóujiàn | e-mail

❶ 警察局 | police station
jǐngchájú

❷ 便衣警察 | plainclothes officer
biànyī jǐngchá

❸ 交通警察 | traffic officer
jiāotōng jǐngchá

❹ 警帽 | police hat
jǐngmào

❺ 哨子 | whistle
shàozi

❻ 肩章 | patch
jiānzhāng

❼ 警徽 | badge
jǐnghuī

❽ 手枪 | gun
shǒuqiāng

❾ 腰带 | duty belt
yāodài

❿ 警棍 | police baton
jǐnggùn

⓫ 手铐 | handcuffs
shǒukào

⑫ 小偷 | thief
xiǎotōu

⑬ 巡警 | patrol officer
xúnjǐng

⑭ 警犬 | police dog
jǐngquǎn

⑮ 警用摩托车 | police motorcycle
jǐngyòng mótuōchē

⑯ 巡逻车 | patrol car
xúnluóchē

⑰ 报警 | call the police
bàojǐng

⑱ 笔录 | written report
bǐlù

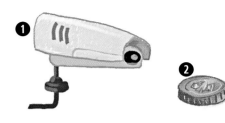

❶ 监视器 | security camera
jiānshìqì

❷ 硬币 | coin
yìngbì

❸ 纸钞 | bill
zhǐchāo

❹ 保险箱 | safe
bǎoxiǎnxiāng

❺ 保险柜 | safe-deposit box
bǎoxiǎnguì

❻ 窗口 | counter
chuāngkǒu

❼ 提款 | withdrawal
tíkuǎn

❽ 银行出纳员 | teller
yínháng chūnàyuán

❾ 外币兑换 | currency exchange
wàibì duìhuàn

❿ 警铃 | alarm
jǐnglíng

⓫ 存款 | deposit
cúnkuǎn

⓬ 自动提款机 | ATM
zìdòng tíkuǎnjī

⓭ 保安 | security guard
bǎo'ān

84

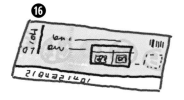

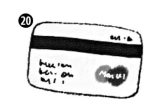

⑭ 运钞车 yùnchāochē	armored truck	⑮ 股票 gǔpiào	stock	⑯ 汇票 huìpiào	money order	⑰ 支票 zhīpiào	check
⑱ 旅行支票 lǚxíng zhīpiào	traveler's check	⑲ 存折 cúnzhé	passbook	⑳ 银行卡 yínhángkǎ	ATM card	㉑ 信用卡 xìnyòngkǎ	credit card
㉒ 身分证 shēnfènzhèng	identity card	㉓ 居留证 jūliúzhèng	residence permit	㉔ 印章 yìnzhāng	official seal	㉕ 签名 qiānmíng	signature

❶ 电梯
diàntī
elevator

❷ 展示柜
zhǎnshìguì
display counter

❸ 店员
diànyuán
salesclerk

❹ 女装部
nǚzhuāngbù
women's department

❺ 内衣部
nèiyībù
lingerie department

❻ 失物招领处
shīwù zhāolǐngchù
lost-and-found center

❼ 自动扶梯
zìdòng fútī
escalator

❽ 家电部
jiādiànbù
household appliances department

❾ 小家电部
xiǎojiādiànbù
home electronics department

❿ 家具部
jiājùbù
home furnishing department

⓫ 青少年服饰部
qīngshàonián fúshìbù
teen department

⓬ 运动器材部
yùndòng qìcáibù
sporting-goods department

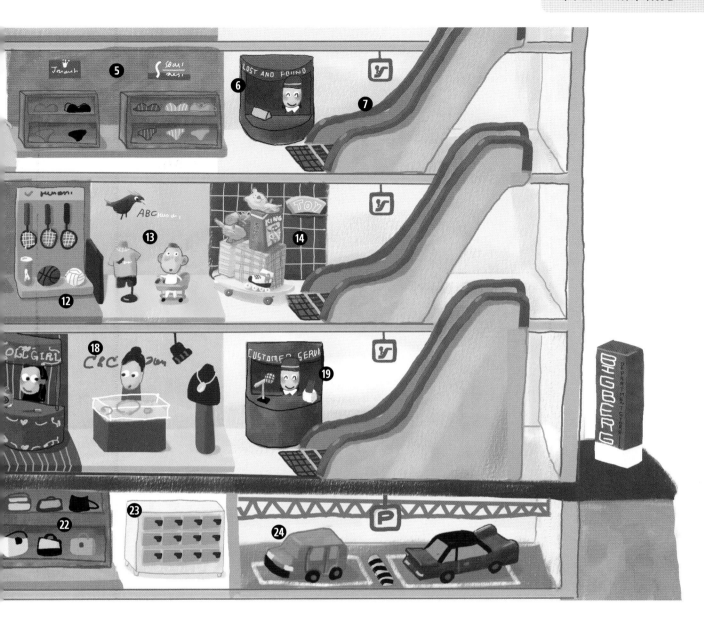

<table>
<tr>
<td>

⑬ 童装部
tóngzhuāngbù

</td>
<td>children's department</td>
<td>

⑭ 玩具部
wánjùbù

</td>
<td>toy department</td>
<td>

⑮ 男装部
nánzhuāngbù

</td>
<td>men's department</td>
</tr>
<tr>
<td>

⑯ 问讯处
wènxùnchù

</td>
<td>information desk</td>
<td>

⑰ 化妆品部
huàzhuāngpǐnbù

</td>
<td>cosmetics department</td>
<td>

⑱ 珠宝区
zhūbǎoqū

</td>
<td>jewelry department</td>
</tr>
<tr>
<td>

⑲ 服务台
fúwùtái

</td>
<td>customer service center</td>
<td>

⑳ 鞋类区
xiélèiqū

</td>
<td>shoe department</td>
<td>

㉑ 美食区
měishíqū

</td>
<td>food court</td>
</tr>
<tr>
<td>

㉒ 皮件部
píjiànbù

</td>
<td>leather goods department</td>
<td>

㉓ 置物柜
zhìwùguì

</td>
<td>lockers</td>
<td>

㉔ 地下停车场
dìxià tíngchēchǎng

</td>
<td>underground parking garage</td>
</tr>
</table>

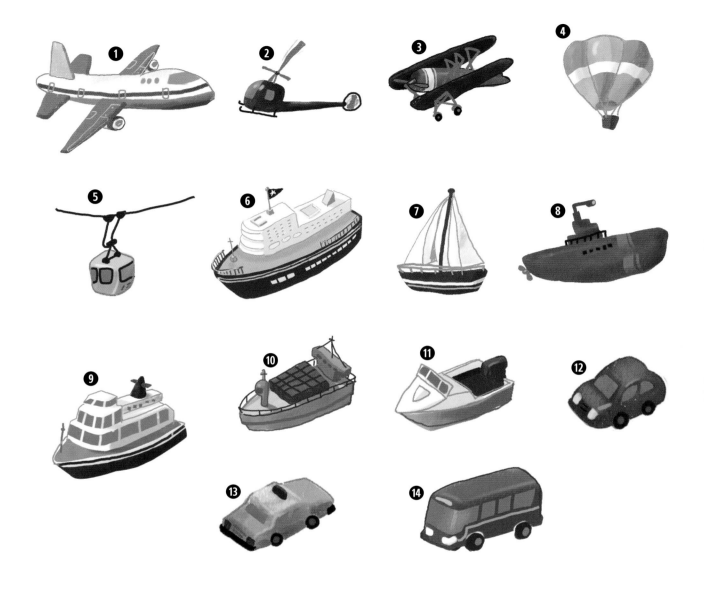

❶ 大型喷气式客机 | jumbo jet
dàxíng pēnqìshì kèjī

❷ 直升机 | helicopter
zhíshēngjī

❸ 双翼飞机 | biplane
shuāngyì fēijī

❹ 热气球 | hot-air balloon
rèqìqiú

❺ 缆车 | cable car
lǎnchē

❻ 游轮 | ocean liner
yóulún

❼ 帆船 | sailboat
fānchuán

❽ 潜水艇 | submarine
qiánshuǐtǐng

❾ 渡轮 | ferry
dùlún

❿ 货柜船 | container ship
huòguìchuán

⓫ 汽艇 | motorboat
qìtǐng

⓬ 轿车 | sedan
jiàochē

⓭ 出租车 | taxi
chūzūchē

⓮ 游览车 | tour bus
yóulǎnchē

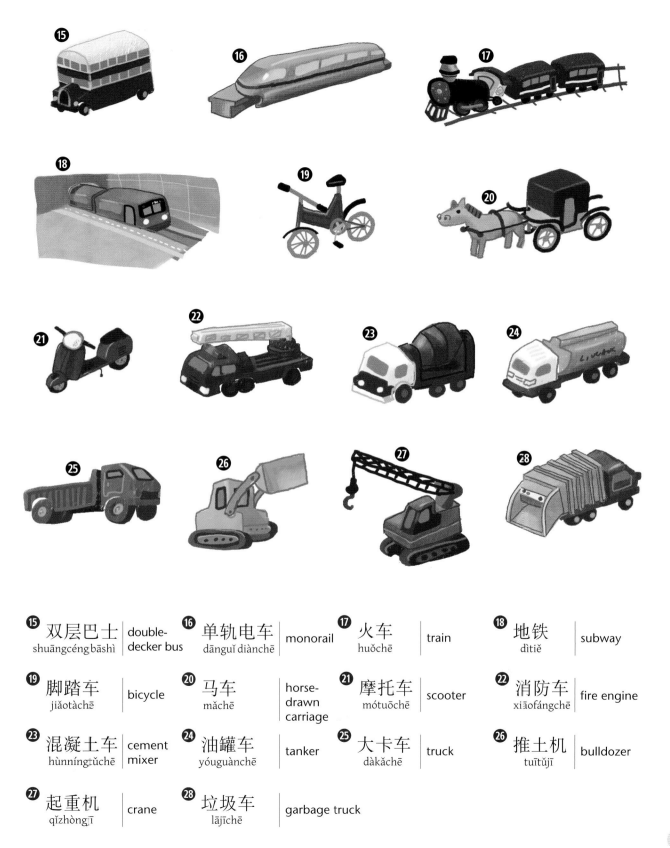

<table>
<tr><td>

15 双层巴士
shuāngcéng bāshì

</td><td>double-decker bus</td><td>

16 单轨电车
dānguǐ diànchē

</td><td>monorail</td><td>

17 火车
huǒchē

</td><td>train</td><td>

18 地铁
dìtiě

</td><td>subway</td></tr>
</table>

15 双层巴士 shuāngcéng bāshì | double-decker bus
16 单轨电车 dānguǐ diànchē | monorail
17 火车 huǒchē | train
18 地铁 dìtiě | subway

19 脚踏车 jiǎotàchē | bicycle
20 马车 mǎchē | horse-drawn carriage
21 摩托车 mótuōchē | scooter
22 消防车 xiāofángchē | fire engine

23 混凝土车 hùnníngtǔchē | cement mixer
24 油罐车 yóuguànchē | tanker
25 大卡车 dàkǎchē | truck
26 推土机 tuītǔjī | bulldozer

27 起重机 qǐzhòngjī | crane
28 垃圾车 lājīchē | garbage truck

❶ 公园
gōngyuán
| park

❷ 天桥
tiānqiáo
| pedestrian bridge

❸ 拐角（处）
guǎijiǎo (chù)
| corner

❹ 道路标示
dàolù biāoshì
| street sign

❺ 地铁入口
dìtiě rùkǒu
| subway entrance

❻ 马路
mǎlù
| road

❼ 人行道
rénxíngdào
| sidewalk

❽ 站牌
zhànpái
| bus stop

❾ 加油站
jiāyóuzhàn
| gas station

❿ 高速公路
gāosù gōnglù
| freeway

⓫ 十字路口
shízì lùkǒu
| intersection

⓬ 人行横道
rénxíng héngdào
| crosswalk

⓭ 路灯
lùdēng
| streetlight

⓮ 红绿灯
hóng-lùdēng
| traffic light

⓯ 骑楼
qílóu
| arcade

⓰ 地下通道
dìxià tōngdào
| underpass

⓱ 马路牙子
mǎlù yázi
| curb

⓲ 停车位
tíngchēwèi
| parking space

❶ 盥洗室 | lavatory
guànxǐshì

❷ 空中小姐／ | flight attendant
kōngzhōng xiǎojiě／
空中先生
kōngzhōng xiānsheng

❸ 紧急出口 | emergency exit
jǐnjí chūkǒu

❹ 遮阳板 | window blind
zhēyángbǎn

❺ 折叠餐桌 | tray
zhé-diécānzhuō

❻ 置物袋 | seat pocket
zhìwùdài

❼ 救生衣 | life preserver
jiùshēngyī

❽ 置物柜 | overhead compartment
zhìwùguì

❾ 靠窗座位 | window seat
kàochuāng zuòwèi

❿ 靠通道座位 | aisle seat
kào tōngdào zuòwèi

⓫ 安全带 | seat belt
ānquándài

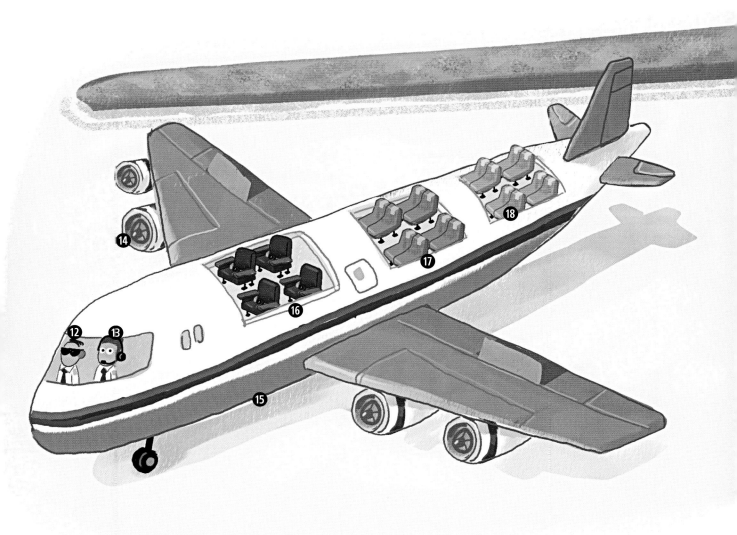

⑫ 副机长 copilot
fùjīzhǎng

⑬ 机长 captain
jīzhǎng

⑭ 喷气发动机 jet engine
pēnqì　fādòngjī

⑮ 飞机机身 fuselage
fēijī jīshēn

⑯ 头等舱 first class
tóuděngcāng

⑰ 商务舱 business class
shāngwùcāng

⑱ 经济舱 economy class
jīngjìcāng

❶ 航站楼 | terminal
hángzhànlóu

❷ 外币兑换处 | currency exchange
wàibì duìhuànchù

❸ 保险柜台 | insurance counter
bǎoxiǎn guìtái

❹ 登机报到柜台 | check-in counter
dēngjī bàodào guìtái

❺ 降落 | landing
jiàngluò

❻ 飞机 | airplane
fēijī

❼ 旅客 | passenger
lǚkè

❽ 地勤人员 | airline representative
dìqín rényuán

❾ 航空公司服务柜台 | airline service counter
hángkōng gōngsī fúwù guìtái

❿ 行李 | luggage
xíngli

⓫ 手推车 | luggage cart
shǒutuīchē

⑫ 行李搬运员 xíngli bānyùnyuán	skycap	⑬ 海关 hǎiguān	customs	⑭ 出入境 chū-rùjìng	immigration	⑮ 行李输送带 xíngli shūsòngdài	luggage carousel
⑯ 出境大厅 chūjìng dàtīng	departure lobby	⑰ 服务台 fúwùtái	information desk	⑱ 塔台 tǎtái	control tower	⑲ 免税商店 miǎnshuì shāngdiàn	duty-free shop
⑳ 免税商品 miǎnshuì shāngpǐn	duty-free item	㉑ 机场巴士 jīchǎng bāshì	shuttle bus	㉒ 跑道 pǎodào	runway	㉓ 起飞 qǐfēi	takeoff

❶ 下国际象棋 xià guójì xiàngqí	play chess	❷ 下象棋 xià xiàngqí	play Chinese chess	❸ 玩儿牌 wánr pái	play cards	❹ 打麻将 dǎ májiàng	play mahjong
❺ 绘画 huìhuà	painting	❻ 雕刻 diāokè	sculpting	❼ 跳舞 tiàowǔ	dancing	❽ 爬山 páshān	hiking
❾ 登山 dēngshān	mountain climbing	❿ 露营 lùyíng	camping	⓫ 钓鱼 diào yú	fishing		

⑫ 园艺 yuányì　gardening	**⑬ 赏鸟** shǎng niǎo　bird-watching	**⑭ 唱卡拉OK** chàng kǎlā-OK　singing karaoke	**⑮ 逛街** guàngjiē　window shopping
⑯ 摄影 shèyǐng　photography	**⑰ 阅读 / 看书** yuèdú / kànshū　reading	**⑱ 听音乐** tīng yīnyuè　listening to music	**⑲ 看电视** kàn diànshì　watching TV
⑳ 看电影 kàn diànyǐng　watching movies	**㉑ 打电子游戏** dǎ diànzǐ yóuxì　playing video games	**㉒ 上网** shàngwǎng　surfing the Internet	

❶ 萨克斯风 | saxophone
sàkèsīfēng

❷ 长笛 | flute
chángdí

❸ 竖笛 | clarinet
shùdí

❹ 双簧管 | oboe
shuānghuángguǎn

❺ 长号 | trombone
chánghào

❻ 法国号 | French horn
Fǎguóhào

❼ 小号 | trumpet
xiǎohào

❽ 大号 | tuba
dàhào

❾ 口琴 | harmonica
kǒuqín

❿ 吉他 | guitar
jítā

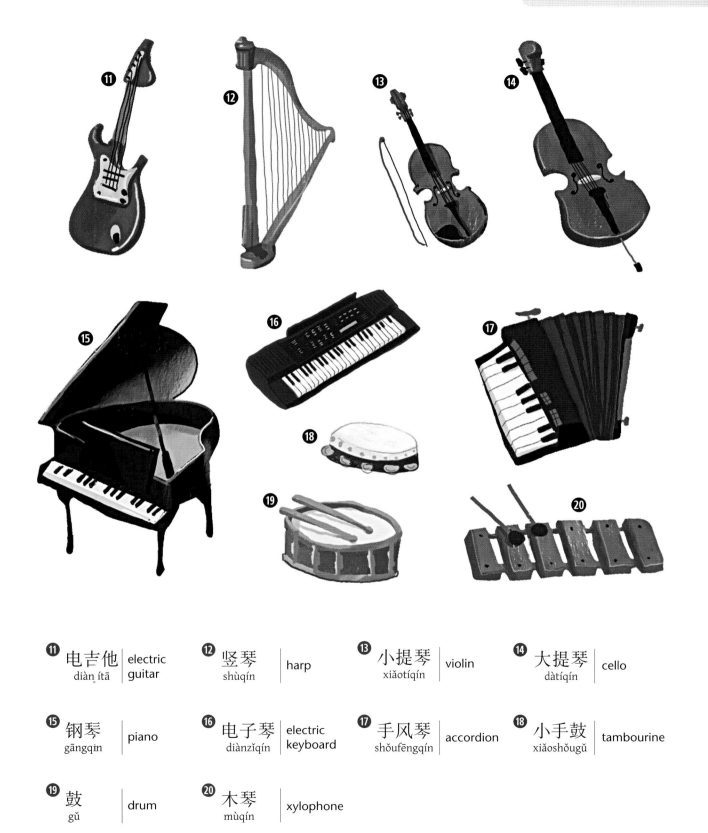

⑪ 电吉他 diàn jítā | electric guitar

⑫ 竖琴 shùqín | harp

⑬ 小提琴 xiǎotíqín | violin

⑭ 大提琴 dàtíqín | cello

⑮ 钢琴 gāngqín | piano

⑯ 电子琴 diànzǐqín | electric keyboard

⑰ 手风琴 shǒufēngqín | accordion

⑱ 小手鼓 xiǎoshǒugǔ | tambourine

⑲ 鼓 gǔ | drum

⑳ 木琴 mùqín | xylophone

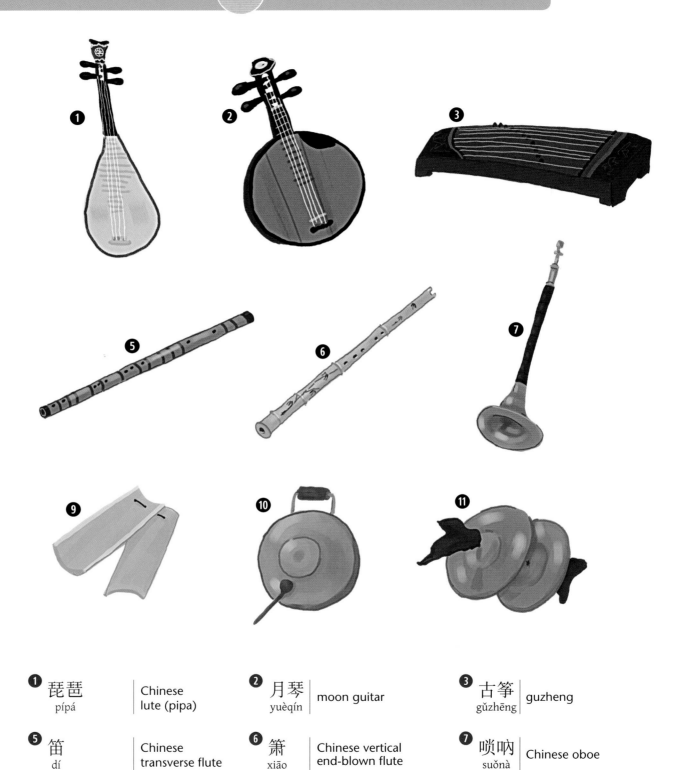

❶ 琵琶 pípá	Chinese lute (pipa)	**❷ 月琴** yuèqín	moon guitar	**❸ 古筝** gǔzhēng	guzheng
❺ 笛 dí	Chinese transverse flute	**❻ 箫** xiāo	Chinese vertical end-blown flute	**❼ 唢呐** suǒnà	Chinese oboe
❾ 拍板 / 鼓板 pāibǎn / gǔbǎn	clapper	**❿ 锣** luó	gong	**⓫ 钹** bó	cymbals

Cultural Window

Chinese Music Played with a Western Twist - The Butterfly Lovers' Violin Concerto

The Butterfly Lovers' Violin Concerto is one of China's musical masterpieces. The concerto was composed by two students, He Zhanhao and Chen Gang, from Shanghai Conservatory of Music in 1958. The Concerto's melody was based on the Shaoxing Opera "Butterfly Love Story." They integrated western and eastern style music by imitating the solo part of the "Erhu" from the opera with a violin. The violin lent itself well to this dismal yet beautiful love story. The Concerto was later arranged into still other versions, such as a piano and a "Pipa" concerto, and was also performed by numerous musicians. If you have the chance to experience it, don't miss the sublime, heart stirring melody of The Butterfly Lovers' Violin Concerto.

A Chinese Love Story

The Butterfly Love Story is a profoundly affecting love story between Liang Shanbo (Liang) and Zhu Yingtai (Zhu). Zhu disguised herself as a man so she could study in Hangzhou. On her journey to school she met Liang, who was to be her classmate. During their three years of shared academic life Zhu and Liang developed a strong friendship. Zhu had romantic feelings for Liang too, but she hid her feelings. After her studies, she returned home. When Liang came to visit her, he discovered her true gender. He was overjoyed and proposed to Zhu, but Zhu's father had already promised her to another man (Ma Wencai). Liang was heartbroken and sank into a depression so severe it took his life. On the day Zhu was traveling to her wedding, she passed by Liang's grave. A strong wind stopped the wedding procession. Zhu left the procession to pay respect to Liang, and his grave suddenly collapsed. Zhu jumped in and was swallowed by the earth. After a while, a pair of colorful butterflies rose from the grave and flew away.

❹ 二胡
　èrhú | Chinese violin (erhu)

❽ 笙
　shēng | reed pipe wind instrument

⓬ 大鼓
　dàgǔ | Chinese drum

Additional Information: Symptoms

1. 发烧 fāshāo | fever
2. 感冒 gǎnmào | cold
3. 咳嗽 késou | cough
4. 头晕 tóuyūn | dizzy
5. 胃疼 wèiténg | stomachache
6. 头疼 tóuténg | headache
7. 嗓子疼 sǎngziténg | sore throat
8. 牙疼 yáténg | toothache
9. 背疼 bèiténg | backache

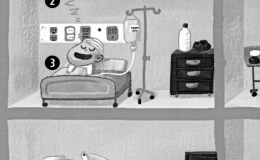

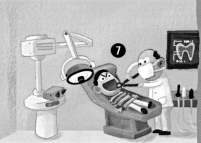

❶ 救护车 jiùhùchē	ambulance	❷ 病房 bìngfáng	ward	❸ 病人 bìngrén	patient	❹ 耳鼻喉科大夫 ěrbíhóukē dàifu	ear, nose, and throat doctor
❺ 手术室 shǒushùshì	operating room	❻ 加护病房 jiāhù bìngfáng	ICU	❼ 牙科大夫 yákē dàifu	dentist	❽ 儿科大夫 érkē dàifu	pediatrician
❾ 产科大夫 chǎnkē dàifu	obstetrician	❿ 眼科大夫 yǎnkē dàifu	ophthalmologist	⓫ 内科大夫 nèikē dàifu	internal medicine specialist	⓬ 外科大夫 wàikē dàifu	surgeon

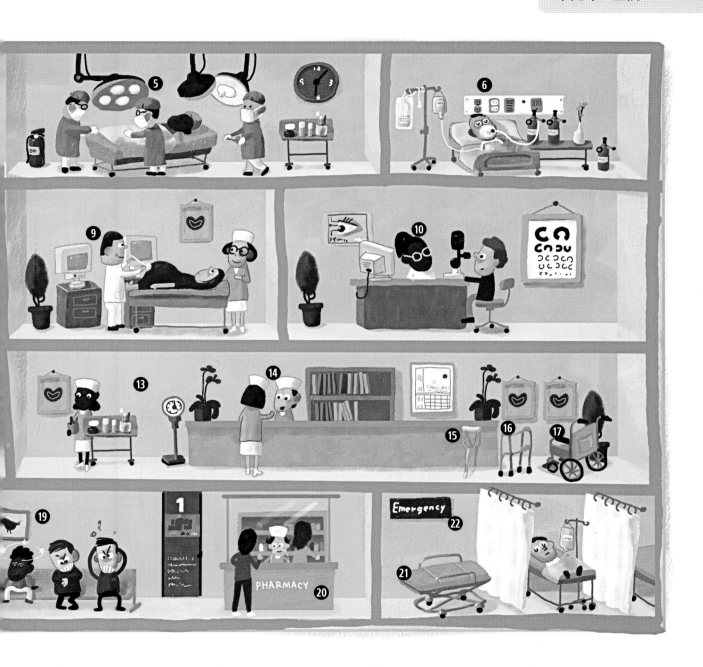

13 护理室 hùlǐshì | nurse's station

14 护士 hùshi | nurse

15 拐杖 guǎizhàng | crutch

16 步行器 bùxíngqì | walker

17 轮椅 lúnyǐ | wheelchair

18 挂号处 guàhàochù | reception

19 候诊室 hòuzhěnshì | waiting room

20 药房 yàofáng | pharmacy

21 担架 dānjià | stretcher

22 急诊室 jízhěnshì | emergency room

❶ 钵 / mortar
bō

❷ 钵槌 / pestle
bōchuí

❸ 中药 / Chinese herbal medicine
zhōngyào

❹ 经络 / meridian
jīngluò

❺ 中医 / Chinese medical doctor
zhōngyī

❻ 把脉 / pulse diagnosis
bǎmài

❼ 穴道 / acupuncture point
xuédào

❽ 气功 / Qigong
qìgōng

❾ 打坐 / meditation
dǎzuò

❿ 推拿 tuīná | Chinese massage

⓫ 膏药 gāoyào | medicinal patch

⓬ 拔罐儿 báguànr | cupping method

⓭ 针灸 zhēnjiǔ | acupuncture

❶ 小学
xiǎoxué
| elementary school

❷ 幼儿园
yòu'éryuán
| kindergarten

❸ 高中
gāozhōng
| senior high school

❹ 初中
chūzhōng
| junior high school

❺ 大学
dàxué
| university

❻ 学士
xuéshì
| Bachelors graduate

❼ 硕士
shuòshì
| Masters graduate

❽ 博士
bóshì
| Doctoral graduate

❾ 研究生院
yánjiùshēngyuàn
| graduate school

❿ 补习班
bǔxíbān
| cram school

Additional Information: School-Related Vocabulary

1. 公立学校 gōnglì xuéxiào	public school	2. 私立学校 sīlì xuéxiào	private school
3. 校长 xiàozhǎng	principal	4. 董事 dǒngshì	director
5. 院长 yuànzhǎng	dean	6. 系主任 xìzhǔrèn	chairman
7. 学者 xuézhě	scholar	8. 校友 xàoyǒu	alumnus
9. 新生 xīnshēng	freshman	10. 年级 niánjí	grade

❶ 运动场 | field
yùndòngchǎng

❷ 跑道 | track
pǎodào

❸ 篮球场 | basketball court
lánqiúchǎng

❹ 校园 | schoolyard
xiàoyuán

❺ 铜像 | bronze statue
tóngxiàng

❻ 校门 | school gate
xiàomén

❼ 布告栏 | bulletin board
bùgàolán

❽ 办公室 | office
bàngōngshì

❾ 校长室 | principal's office
xiàozhǎngshì

❿ 洗手间 | restroom
xǐshǒujiān

⓫ 教室 | classroom
jiàoshì

⓬ 语言实验室 | language lab
yǔyán shíyànshì

⓭ 化学实验室 | chemistry lab
huàxué shíyànshì

⓮ 置物柜 | lockers
zhìwùguì

⓯ 走廊 | hallway
zǒuláng

⓰ 礼堂 | auditorium
lǐtáng

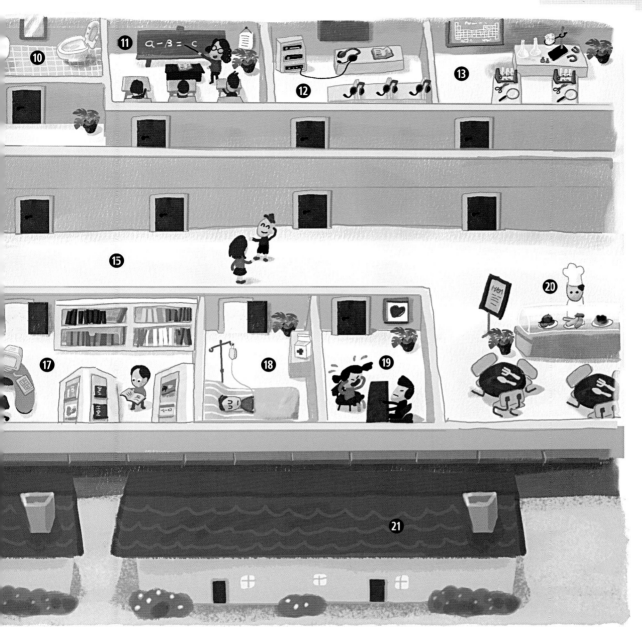

⑰ 图书馆 túshūguǎn | library

⑱ 保健室 bǎojiànshì | nurse's office

⑲ 心理辅导室 xīnlǐ fǔdǎoshì | guidance counselor's office

⑳ 食堂 shítáng | cafeteria

㉑ 宿舍 sùshè | dormitory

Additional Information: Sporting Venues

1. **棒球场** bàngqiúchǎng | baseball field

2. **足球场** zúqiúchǎng | football field / soccer field

3. **保龄球馆** bǎolíngqiúguǎn | bowling alley

4. **网球场** wǎngqiúchǎng | tennis court

5. **高尔夫球场** gāo'ěrfūqiúchǎng | golf course

6. **羽毛球场** yǔmáoqiúchǎng | badminton court

7. **体育馆** tǐyùguǎn | gym

Part I Courses · 课程

① 课程表 kèchéngbiǎo | timetable

② 科目 kēmù | subject

③ 中文 Zhōngwén | Chinese

④ 英文 Yīngwén | English

⑤ 日文 Rìwén | Japanese

⑥ 外语 wàiyǔ | foreign language

⑦ 语言学 yǔyánxué | linguistics

⑧ 哲学 zhéxué | philosophy

⑨ 文学 wénxué | literature

⑩ 数学 shùxué | math

⑪ 经济 jīngjì | economics

⑫ 商业 shāngyè | business

⑬ 工程 gōngchéng | engineering

⑭ 建筑 jiànzhù | architecture

⑮ 地理 dìlǐ | geography

⑯ 历史 lìshǐ | history

⑰ 天文 tiānwén | astronomy

⑱ 物理 wùlǐ | physics

⑲ 化学 huàxué | chemistry

⑳ 生物 shēngwù | biology

㉑ 医学 yīxué | medicine

㉒ 法律 fǎlǜ | law

㉓ 政治学 zhèngzhìxué | political science

㉔ 社会学 shèhuìxué | sociology

㉕ 音乐 yīnyuè | music

㉖ 体育 tǐyù | physical education

Part II   Campus Life · 校园生活

❶ 学期
xuéqī
| semester

❷ 作业
zuòyè
| homework

❸ 作文
zuòwén
| essay

❹ 考试
kǎoshì
| exam

❺ 月考
yuèkǎo
| monthly test

❻ 期中考试
qīzhōng kǎoshì
| midterm

❼ 期末考试
qīmò kǎoshì
| final exam

❽ 口头报告
kǒutóu bàogào
| oral presentation

❾ 小组讨论
xiǎozǔ tǎolùn
| group discussion

❿ 听写
tīngxiě
| dictation

⓫ 作弊
zuòbì
| cheat

⓬ 不及格
bùjígé
| fail

⓭ 奖学金
jiǎngxuéjīn
| scholarship

⓮ 社团活动
shètuán huódòng
| club activity

⓯ 打工
dǎgōng
| part-time job

⓰ 毕业
bìyè
| graduation

❶ 黑板
hēibǎn | blackboard

❷ 粉笔
fěnbǐ | chalk

❸ 黑板擦
hēibǎncā | eraser

❹ 讲台
jiǎngtái | platform

❺ 橡皮
xiàngpí | eraser

❻ 写字垫板
xiězì diànbǎn | desk mat

❼ 铅笔盒
qiānbǐhé | pencil box

❽ 麦克风
màikèfēng | microphone

❾ 投影机
tóuyǐngjī | projector

❿ 教科书
jiàokēshū | textbook

⓫ 桌子
zhuōzi | desk

⓬ 椅子
yǐzi | chair

⓭ 地球仪
dìqiúyí | globe

⓮ 地图
dìtú | map

⓯ 书架
shūjià | bookrack

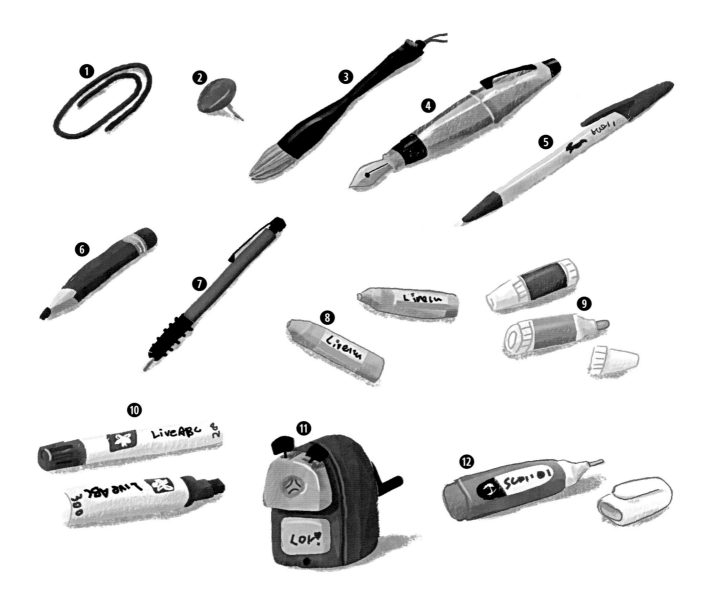

❶ 回形针 | paper clip
huíxíngzhēn

❷ 图钉 | thumbtack
túdīng

❸ 毛笔 | calligraphy brush
máobǐ

❹ 钢笔 | fountain pen
gāngbǐ

❺ 圆珠笔 | ballpoint pen
yuánzhūbǐ

❻ 铅笔 | pencil
qiānbǐ

❼ 自动铅笔 | mechanical pencil
zìdòng qiānbǐ

❽ 蜡笔 | crayon
làbǐ

❾ 彩笔 | color pen
cǎibǐ

❿ 记号笔 | marker
jìhàobǐ

⓫ 铅笔刀 | pencil sharpener
qiānbǐdāo

⓬ 修正液 | white-out
xiūzhèngyè

⑬ 尺子 chǐzi | ruler	**⑭ 圆规** yuánguī | compass	**⑮ 订书器** dìngshūqì | stapler	**⑯ 剪刀** jiǎndāo | scissors
⑰ 胶水 jiāoshuǐ | glue	**⑱ 调色盘** tiáosèpán | paint palette	**⑲ 颜料** yánliào | paint	**⑳ 墨水** mòshuǐ | ink
㉑ 笔记本 bǐjìběn | notebook	**㉒ 活页纸** huóyèzhǐ | binder paper	**㉓ 文件夹** wénjiànjiá | folder	

❶ 红色 | red
hóngsè

❷ 粉红色 | pink
fěnhóngsè

❸ 橘色 | orange
júsè

❹ 黄色 | yellow
huángsè

❺ 绿色 | green
lǜsè

❻ 蓝色 | blue
lánsè

❼ 紫色 | purple
zǐsè

❽ 咖啡色 | brown
kāfēisè

❾ 黑色 | black
hēisè

❿ 白色 | white
báisè

⓫ 灰色 | gray
huīsè

⓬ 米色 | creamy white
mǐsè

⓭ 银色 | silver
yínsè

⓮ 金色 | gold
jīnsè

⓯ 深色 | dark
shēnsè

⓰ 浅色 | light
qiǎnsè

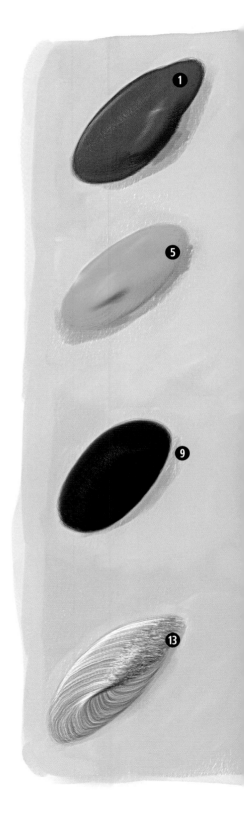

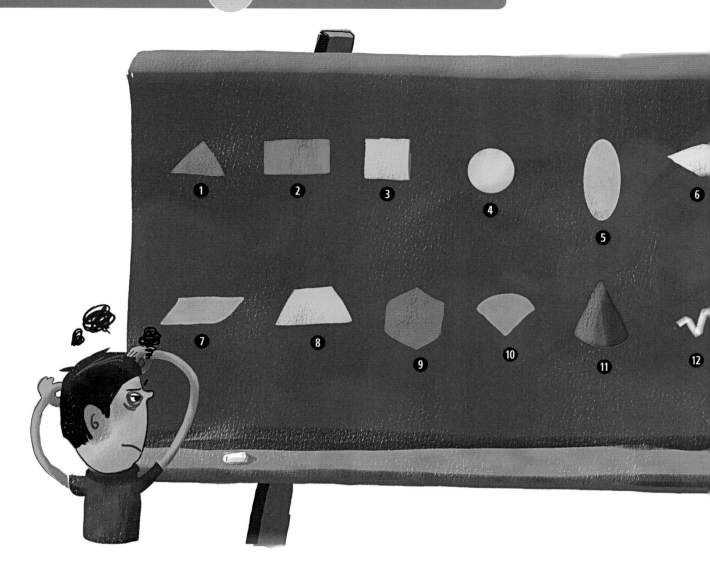

① 三角形 sānjiǎoxíng | triangle

② 矩形 jǔxíng | rectangle

③ 正方形 zhèngfāngxíng | square

④ 圆形 yuánxíng | circle

⑤ 椭圆形 tuǒyuánxíng | oval

⑥ 菱形 língxíng | diamond

⑦ 平行四边形 píngxíng sìbiānxíng | parallelogram

⑧ 梯形 tīxíng | trapezoid

⑨ 多角形 duōjiǎoxíng | polygon

⑩ 扇形 shànxíng | sector

⑪ 圆锥体 yuánzhuītǐ | cone

⑫ 平方根 píngfānggēn | square root symbol

⑬ 加号 jiāhào | plus sign

⑭ 减号 jiǎnhào | minus sign

⑮ 乘号 chénghào | multiplication sign

⑯ 除号 chúhào | division sign

⑰ 大于号 dàyúhào | greater than sign

⑱ 小于号 xiǎoyúhào | less than sign

⑲ 等号 děnghào | equal sign

⑳ 惊叹号 jīngtànhào | exclamation point

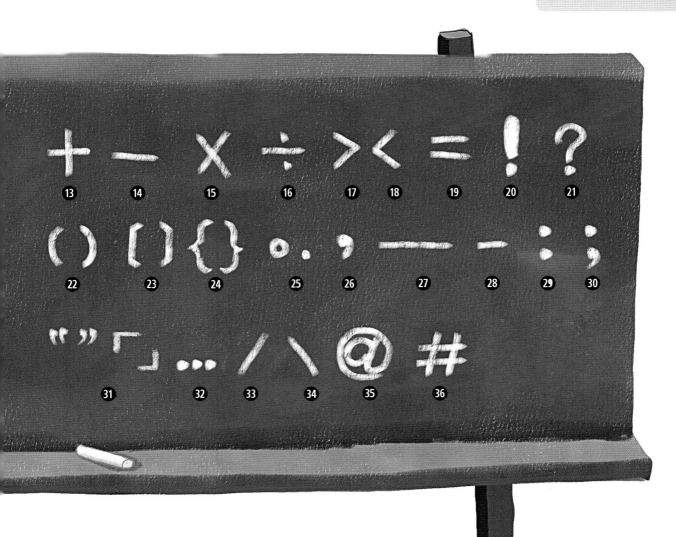

㉑ 问号 wènhào	question mark	㉒ 小括号 xiǎokuòhào	parentheses	㉓ 方括号 fāngkuòhào	brackets	㉔ 大括号 dàkuòhào	braces
㉕ 句号 jùhào	period	㉖ 逗号 dòuhào	comma	㉗ 破折号 pòzhéhào	dash	㉘ 连字符 liánzìfú	hyphen
㉙ 冒号 màohào	colon	㉚ 分号 fēnhào	semicolon	㉛ 引号 yǐnhào	quotation marks	㉜ 省略号 shěnglüèhào	ellipsis
㉝ 左斜线 zuǒxiéxiàn	slash	㉞ 右斜线 yòuxiéxiàn	backslash	㉟ at	at symbol	㊱ 井号 jínghào	pound sign

❶ 跳伞 tiàosǎn	skydiving	❷ 玩儿滑翔翼 wánr huáxiángyì	hang gliding	❸ 划船 huáchuán	boating	❹ 漂流 piāoliú	white-water rafting
❺ 游泳 yóuyǒng	swimming	❻ 花样滑冰 huāyàng huábīng	figure skating	❼ 滑冰 huábīng	ice-skating	❽ 溜旱冰/ liū hànbīng/ 滑旱冰 huá hànbīng	roller skating
❾ 滚轴溜冰 gǔnzhóu liūbīng	in-line skating						

⑩ 射箭
shèjiàn | archery

⑪ 慢跑
mànpǎo | jogging

⑫ 骑自行车
qí zìxíngchē | cycling

⑬ 骑马
qímǎ | horseback riding

⑭ 玩儿滑板
wánr huábǎn | skateboarding

⑮ 单板滑雪
dānbǎn huáxuě | snowboarding

⑯ 滑雪
huáxuě | skiing

⑰ 攀岩
pānyán | rock climbing

❶ 保龄球 bǎolíngqiú	bowling	**❷ 篮球** lánqiú	basketball	

❶ 保龄球 bǎolíngqiú | bowling   **❷ 篮球** lánqiú | basketball   **❸ 手球** shǒuqiú | handball   **❹ 棒球** bàngqiú | baseball

❺ 躲避球 duǒbìqiú | dodgeball   **❻ 高尔夫球** gāo'ěrfūqiú | golf   **❼ 网球** wǎngqiú | tennis   **❽ 垒球** lěiqiú | softball

❾ 乒乓球 pīngpāngqiú | table tennis   **❿ 冰球** bīngqiú | ice hockey

⑪ 曲棍球 | field hockey
qūgùnqiú

⑫ 足球 | soccer
zúqiú

⑬ 美式足球 | American
Měishì zúqiú | football

⑭ 槌球 | croquet
chuíqiú

⑮ 台球 | pool
táiqiú

⑯ 排球 | volleyball
páiqiú

⑰ 羽毛球 | badminton
yǔmáoqiú

⑱ 板球 | cricket
bǎnqiú

⑲ 壁球 | squash
bìqiú

❶ 狗爬 | dog paddle
gǒupá

❷ 蛙泳 | breaststroke
wāyǒng

❸ 自由泳 | freestyle
zìyóuyǒng

❹ 仰泳 | backstroke
yǎngyǒng

❺ 蝶泳 | butterfly stroke
diéyǒng

❻ 侧泳 | sidestroke
cèyǒng

❼ 跳水 | dive
tiàoshuǐ

❽ 水上芭蕾 | synchronized swimming
shuǐshàng bāléi

❾ 滑水 huáshuǐ	waterskiing	❿ 冲浪 chōnglàng	surfing	⓫ 浮板运动 fúbǎn yùndòng	kickboarding	⓬ 帆板 fānbǎn	windsurfing
⓭ 水上摩托 shuǐshàng mótuō	jet skiing	⓮ 浮潜 fúqián	snorkeling	⓯ 潜水 qiánshuǐ	scuba diving		

❶ 掷链球 | hammer throw
zhì liànqiú

❷ 掷铁饼 | discus throw
zhì tiěbǐng

❸ 推铅球 | shot put
tuī qiānqiú

❹ 跳远 | long jump
tiàoyuǎn

❺ 跳高 | high jump
tiàogāo

❻ 三级跳 | triple jump
sānjítiào

❼ 跨栏 | hurdles
kuàlán

❽ 撑竿跳 | pole vault
chēnggāntiào

9 掷标枪
zhì biāociāng | javelin throw

10 障碍赛跑
zhàng'ài sàipǎo | steeplechase

11 马拉松
mǎlāsōng | marathon

12 接力赛
jiēlìsài | relay race

13 短跑
duǎnpǎo | sprint

14 百米短跑
bǎimǐ duǎnpǎo | hundred-meter dash

15 跑道
pǎodào | track

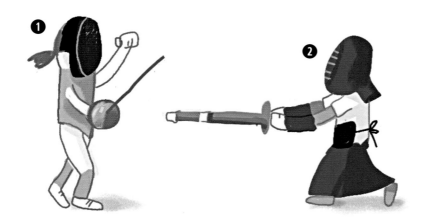

❶ 西洋剑	fencing	**❷ 剑道**	kendo	**❸ 太极拳**	tai chi
xīyángjiàn		jiàndào		tàijíquán	

❹ 功夫	kung fu	**❺ 合气道**	aikido	**❻ 柔道**	judo
gōngfu		héqìdào		róudào	

❼ 空手道 | karate
kōngshǒudào

❽ 跆拳道 | tae kwon do
táiquándào

❾ 泰拳 | Thai boxing
Tàiquán

❿ 拳击 | boxing
quánjī

⓫ 摔跤 | wrestling
shuāijiāo

⓬ 相扑 | sumo wrestling
xiàngpū

❶ 双杠
shuānggàng | parallel bars

❷ 吊环
diàohuán | rings

❸ 鞍马
ānmǎ | pommel horse

❹ 单杠
dāngàng | horizontal bar

❺ 高低杠
gāodīgàng | uneven bars

❻ 平衡木
pínghéngmù | balance beam

❼ 跳马
tiàomǎ | vaulting horse

8 蹦床 | trampoline
bèngchuáng

9 跳绳 | jump rope
tiàoshéng

10 瑜珈 | yoga
yújiā

11 有氧运动 | aerobics
yǒuyǎng yùndòng

12 体操 | gymnastics
tǐcāo

13 哑铃 | dumbbell
yǎlíng

14 举重 | weight lifting
jǔzhòng

❶ 老鼠 lǎoshǔ | mouse

❷ 松鼠 sōngshǔ | squirrel

❸ 袋鼠 dàishǔ | kangaroo

❹ 蛇 shé | snake

❺ 狗 gǒu | dog

❻ 猫 māo | cat

❼ 兔子 tùzi | rabbit

❽ 猪 zhū | pig

❾ 猴子 hóuzi | monkey

❿ 考拉 kǎolā | koala

⓫ 山羊 shānyáng | goat

⓬ 绵羊 miányáng | sheep

⓭ 乳牛 rǔniú | cow

⓮ 马 mǎ | horse

⓯ 斑马 bānmǎ | zebra

#	中文	拼音	English
⑯	骆驼	luòtuo	camel
⑰	驴子	lǘzi	donkey
⑱	鹿	lù	deer
⑲	长颈鹿	chángjǐnglù	giraffe
⑳	狼	láng	wolf
㉑	狐狸	húli	fox
㉒	犀牛	xīniú	rhinoceros
㉓	河马	hémǎ	hippopotamus
㉔	熊猫	xióngmāo	panda
㉕	熊	xióng	bear
㉖	狮子	shīzi	lion
㉗	老虎	lǎohǔ	tiger
㉘	大象	dàxiàng	elephant
㉙	北极熊	běijíxióng	polar bear

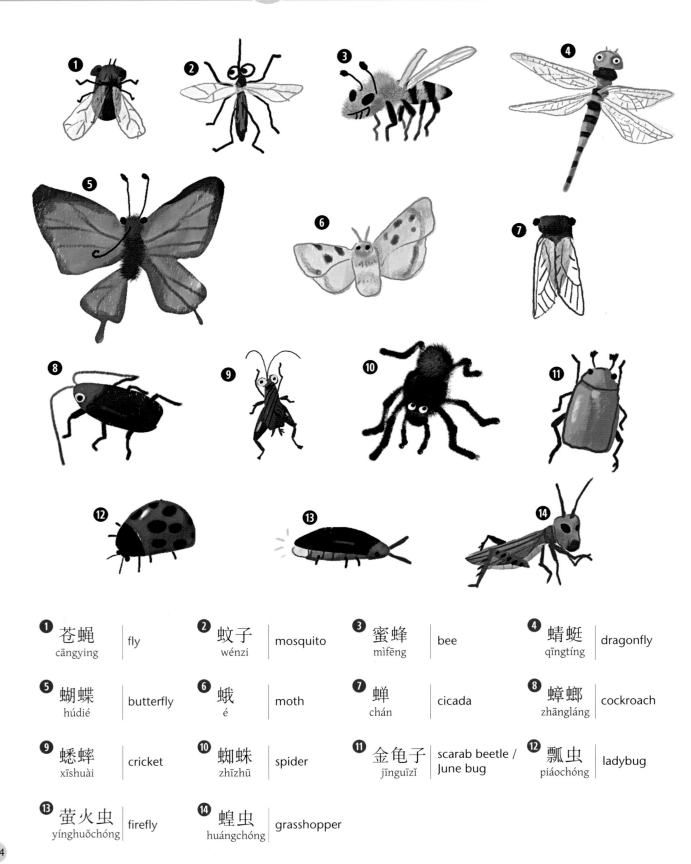

❶ 苍蝇 cāngying | fly

❷ 蚊子 wénzi | mosquito

❸ 蜜蜂 mìfēng | bee

❹ 蜻蜓 qīngtíng | dragonfly

❺ 蝴蝶 húdié | butterfly

❻ 蛾 é | moth

❼ 蝉 chán | cicada

❽ 蟑螂 zhāngláng | cockroach

❾ 蟋蟀 xīshuài | cricket

❿ 蜘蛛 zhīzhū | spider

⓫ 金龟子 jīnguīzǐ | scarab beetle / June bug

⓬ 瓢虫 piáochóng | ladybug

⓭ 萤火虫 yínghuǒchóng | firefly

⓮ 蝗虫 huángchóng | grasshopper

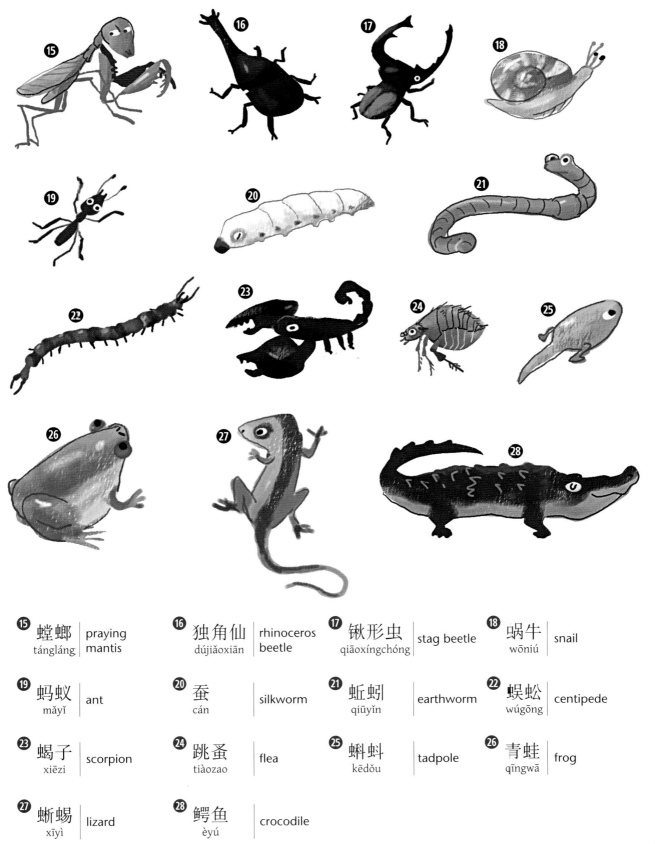

⑮ 螳螂 tángláng	praying mantis	⑯ 独角仙 dújiǎoxiān	rhinoceros beetle	⑰ 锹形虫 qiāoxíngchóng	stag beetle	⑱ 蜗牛 wōniú	snail
⑲ 蚂蚁 mǎyǐ	ant	⑳ 蚕 cán	silkworm	㉑ 蚯蚓 qiūyǐn	earthworm	㉒ 蜈蚣 wúgōng	centipede
㉓ 蝎子 xiēzi	scorpion	㉔ 跳蚤 tiàozao	flea	㉕ 蝌蚪 kēdǒu	tadpole	㉖ 青蛙 qīngwā	frog
㉗ 蜥蜴 xīyì	lizard	㉘ 鳄鱼 èyú	crocodile						

❶ 鸡 jī	chicken	❷ 雉 zhì	pheasant	❸ 鸭子 yāzi	duck	❹ 鹅 é	goose
❺ 天鹅 tiān'é	swan	❻ 企鹅 qǐ'é	penguin	❼ 海鸥 hǎi'ōu	seagull	❽ 白鹭 báilù	egret
❾ 鸽子 gēzi	pigeon	❿ 麻雀 máquè	sparrow	⓫ 啄木鸟 zhuómùniǎo	woodpecker	⓬ 金丝雀 jīnsīquè	canary
⓭ 白文鸟 báiwénniǎo	white Java sparrow	⓮ 乌鸦 wūyā	crow	⓯ 八哥儿 bāger	mynah		

⑯ 鹦鹉 yīngwǔ | parrot	**⑰ 蓝鹊** lánquè | blue magpie	**⑱ 巨嘴鸟** jùzuǐniǎo | toucan	**⑲ 鹈鹕** tíhú | pelican
⑳ 云雀 yúnquè | lark	**㉑ 蜂鸟** fēngniǎo | hummingbird	**㉒ 燕子** yànzi | swallow	**㉓ 伯劳鸟** bóláoniǎo | shrike
㉔ 猫头鹰 māotóuyīng | owl	**㉕ 黑面琵鹭** hēimiànpílù | black-faced spoonbill	**㉖ 鸵鸟** tuóniǎo | ostrich	**㉗ 孔雀** kǒngquè | peacock
㉘ 鹰 yīng | eagle	**㉙ 秃鹰** tūyīng | vulture	**㉚ 秃鹫** tūjiù | condor	

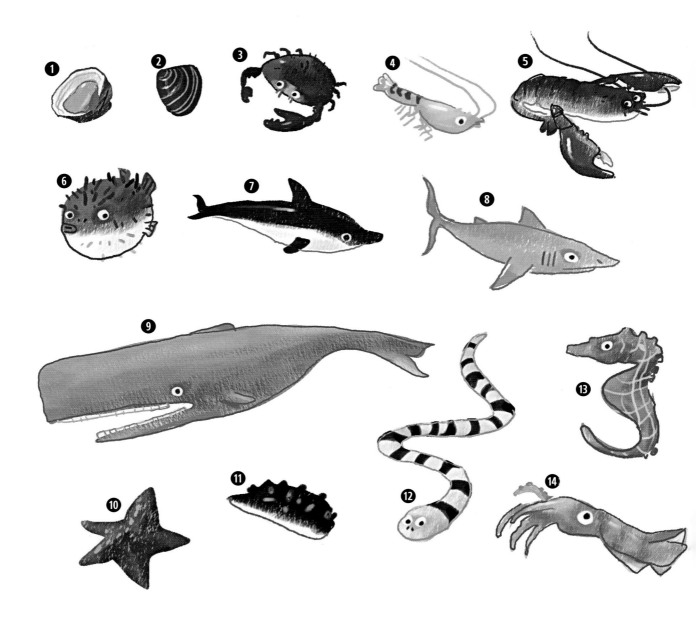

❶	生蚝 shēngháo	oyster	❷	蛤蜊 géli	clam	❸	螃蟹 pángxiè	crab	❹	虾 xiā	shrimp

❶ 生蚝 shēngháo | oyster   **❷ 蛤蜊** géli | clam   **❸ 螃蟹** pángxiè | crab   **❹ 虾** xiā | shrimp

❺ 龙虾 lóngxiā | lobster   **❻ 河豚** hétún | blowfish   **❼ 海豚** hǎitún | dolphin   **❽ 鲨鱼** shāyú | shark

❾ 鲸鱼 jīngyú | whale   **❿ 海星** hǎixīng | starfish   **⓫ 海参** hǎishēn | sea cucumber   **⓬ 海蛇** hǎishé | sea snake

⓭ 海马 hǎimǎ | sea horse   **⓮ 乌贼** wūzéi | squid

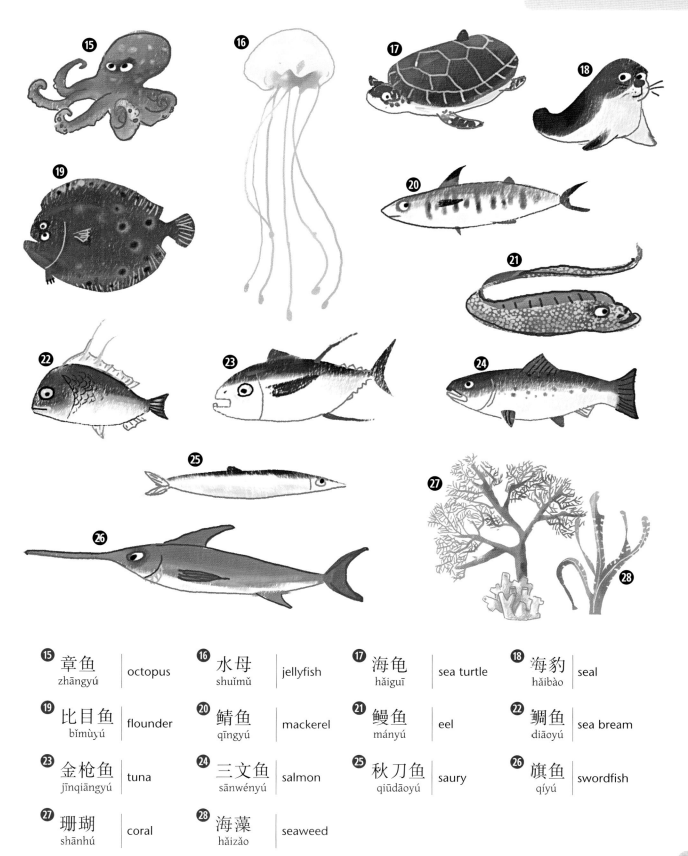

⑮ 章鱼 zhāngyú	octopus	⑯ 水母 shuǐmǔ	jellyfish	⑰ 海龟 hǎiguī	sea turtle	⑱ 海豹 hǎibào	seal
⑲ 比目鱼 bǐmùyú	flounder	⑳ 鲭鱼 qīngyú	mackerel	㉑ 鳗鱼 mányú	eel	㉒ 鲷鱼 diāoyú	sea bream
㉓ 金枪鱼 jīnqiāngyú	tuna	㉔ 三文鱼 sānwényú	salmon	㉕ 秋刀鱼 qiūdāoyú	saury	㉖ 旗鱼 qíyú	swordfish
㉗ 珊瑚 shānhú	coral	㉘ 海藻 hǎizǎo	seaweed						

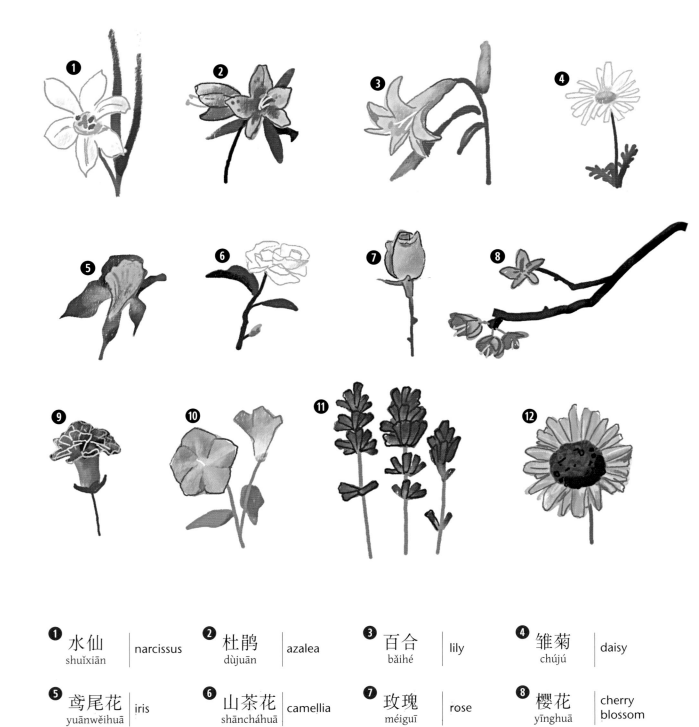

❶ 水仙 shuǐxiān | narcissus	**❷ 杜鹃** dùjuān | azalea	**❸ 百合** bǎihé | lily	**❹ 雏菊** chújú | daisy
❺ 鸢尾花 yuānwěihuā | iris	**❻ 山茶花** shāncháhuā | camellia	**❼ 玫瑰** méiguī | rose	**❽ 樱花** yīnghuā | cherry blossom
❾ 康乃馨 kāngnǎixīn | carnation	**❿ 牵牛花** qiānniúhuā | morning glory	**⓫ 熏衣草** xūnyīcǎo | lavender	**⓬ 向日葵** xiàngrìkuí | sunflower

⑬ 郁金香 yùjīnxāng	tulip	**⑭ 紫罗兰** zǐluólán	violet	**⑮ 油菜花** yóucàihuā	canola	**⑯ 蒲公英** púgōngyīng	dandelion
⑰ 三叶草 sānyècǎo	shamrock	**⑱ 枫叶** fēngyè	maple leaf	**⑲ 圣诞红** shèngdànhóng	poinsettia	**⑳ 蕨类** juélèi	fern
㉑ 柳树 liǔshù	willow	**㉒ 雪松** xuěsōng	cedar	**㉓ 柏树** bóshù	cypress		

❶ 一月 Yīyuè	January	❷ 二月 Èryuè	February	❸ 三月 Sānyuè	March	❹ 四月 Sìyuè	April
❺ 五月 Wǔyuè	May	❻ 六月 Liùyuè	June	❼ 七月 Qīyuè	July	❽ 八月 Bāyuè	August
❾ 九月 Jiǔyuè	September	❿ 十月 Shíyuè	October	⓫ 十一月 Shíyīyuè	November	⓬ 十二月 Shí 'èryuè	December
⓭ 月历 yuèlì	monthly calendar	⓮ 星期日 Xīngqīrì	Sunday	⓯ 星期一 Xīngqīyī	Monday	⓰ 星期二 Xīngqī 'èr	Tuesday
⓱ 星期三 Xīngqīsān	Wednesday	⓲ 星期四 Xīngqīsì	Thursday	⓳ 星期五 Xīngqīwǔ	Friday	⓴ 星期六 Xīngqīliù	Saturday
㉑ 法定假日 fǎdìng jiàrì	national holiday						

Additional Information: Numbers

1. **1** yī / yāo — one	2. **2** èr — two	3. **3** sān — three	4. **4** sì — four	5. **5** wǔ — five	6. **6** liù — six	7. **7** qī — seven
8. **8** bā — eight	9. **9** jiǔ — nine	10. **10** shí — ten	11. **11** shíyī — eleven	12. **12** shí 'èr — twelve	13. **13** shísān — thirteen	14. **14** shísì — fourteen
15. **15** shíwǔ — fifteen	16. **16** shíliù — sixteen	17. **17** shíqī — seventeen	18. **18** shíbā — eighteen	19. **19** shíjiǔ — nineteen	20. **20** èrshí — twenty	21. **30** sānshí — thirty
22. **40** sìshí — forty	23. **50** wǔshí — fifty	24. **一百** yìbǎi — one hundred	25. **一千** yìqiān — one thousand	26. **一万** yíwàn — ten thousand	27. **一亿** yíyì — one hundred million	28. **0** líng — zero

Note:

"1" can sometimes be pronounced as "yāo." Examples are telephone numbers, room numbers, bus and train numbers, etc. In addition, the number needs to be at least three digits and be pronounced digit by digit. For example, room 14 is pronounced as "shísì hào fángjiān" and room 51 is pronounced as "wǔshíyī hào fángjiān" whereas 101 room could be pronounced as "yāo líng yāo hào fángjiān."

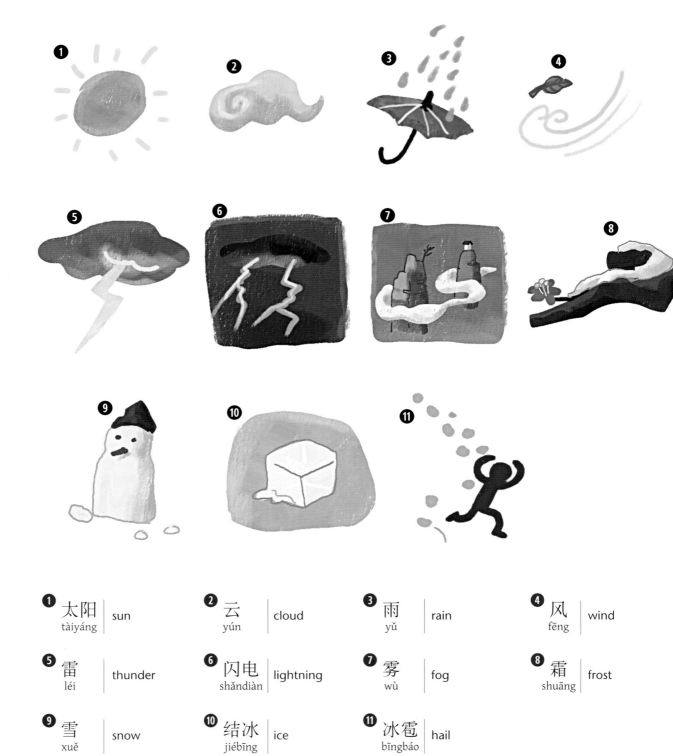

❶ 太阳 tàiyáng | sun

❷ 云 yún | cloud

❸ 雨 yǔ | rain

❹ 风 fēng | wind

❺ 雷 léi | thunder

❻ 闪电 shǎndiàn | lightning

❼ 雾 wù | fog

❽ 霜 shuāng | frost

❾ 雪 xuě | snow

❿ 结冰 jiébīng | ice

⓫ 冰雹 bīngbáo | hail

⓬ 风暴 | storm
fēngbào

⓭ 台风 | typhoon
táifēng

⓮ 龙卷风 | tornado
lóngjuǎnfēng

⓯ 高气压 | high pressure
gāoqìyā

⓰ 冷锋 | cold front
lěngfēng

⓱ 寒流 | cold current
hánliú

⓲ 温度 | temperature
wēndù

⓳ 春天 | spring
chūntiān

⓴ 夏天 | summer
xiàtiān

㉑ 秋天 | fall / autumn
qiūtiān

㉒ 冬天 | winter
dōngtiān

Additional Information: Weather Description

1. 晴天 | sunny day
qíngtiān

2. 阴天 | cloudy day
yīntiān

3. 雨天 | rainy day
yǔtiān

❶ **新年** | New Year
Xīnnián

❷ **除夕** | New Year's Eve
Chúxī

❸ **春节** | Chinese New Year /
Chūnjié | Lunar New Year

❹ **元宵节** | Lantern
Yuánxiāojié | Festival

❺ **清明节** | Tomb-sweeping
Qīngmíngjié | Festival

❻ **端午节** | Dragon
Duānwǔjié | Boat Festival

❼ **中秋节** | Mid-Autumn
Zhōngqiūjié | Festival

❽ **教师节** | Teacher's Day
Jiàoshījié

❾ **情人节** | Valentine's Day
Qíngrénjié

⑩ 劳动节 Láodòngjié | Labor Day

⑪ 国庆节 Guóqìngjié | National Day

⑫ 万圣节 Wànshèngjié | Halloween

⑬ 感恩节 Gǎn'ēnjié | Thanksgiving

⑭ 圣诞节 Shèngdànjié | Christmas

⑮ 母亲节 Mǔqīnjié | Mother's Day

⑯ 父亲节 Fùqīnjié | Father's Day

❶ 高原 gāoyuán	plateau	❷ 森林 sēnlín	forest	❸ 湖 hú	lake	❹ 瀑布 pùbù	waterfall
❺ 山顶 shāndǐng	peak	❻ 山 shān	mountain	❼ 水坝 shuǐbà	dam	❽ 河流 héliú	river
❾ 池塘 chítáng	pond	❿ 树林 shùlín	woods	⓫ 山谷 shāngǔ	valley	⓬ 盆地 péndì	basin

⑬ 平原 píngyuán	plain	⑭ 沙洲 shāzhōu	sandbar	⑮ 海港 hǎigǎng	harbor	⑯ 海滩 hǎitān	beach
⑰ 夕阳 xīyáng	sunset	⑱ 地平线 dìpíngxiàn	horizon	⑲ 岛 dǎo	island	⑳ 海 hǎi	sea

Index

Index

Index